Cambridgeshire

Edited by Laura Rogers

 Young**Writers**

First published in Great Britain in 2005 by:
Young Writers
Remus House
Coltsfoot Drive
Peterborough
PE2 9JX
Telephone: 01733 890066
Website: www.youngwriters.co.uk

SB ISBN 1 84602 156 1

Foreword

Young Writers was established in 1991 and has been passionately devoted to the promotion of reading and writing in children and young adults ever since. The quest continues today. Young Writers remains as committed to the fostering of burgeoning poetic and literary talent as ever.

This year's Young Writers competition has proven as vibrant and dynamic as ever and we are delighted to present a showcase of the best poetry from across the UK. Each poem has been carefully selected from a wealth of *Playground Poets* entries before ultimately being published in this, our thirteenth primary school poetry series.

Once again, we have been supremely impressed by the overall high quality of the entries we have received. The imagination, energy and creativity which has gone into each young writer's entry made choosing the best poems a challenging and often difficult but ultimately hugely rewarding task - the general high standard of the work submitted amply vindicating this opportunity to bring their poetry to a larger appreciative audience.

We sincerely hope you are pleased with our final selection and that you will enjoy *Playground Poets Cambridgeshire* for many years to come.

Contents

Joseph Bradley (8)	14
Scarlett Andrews (7)	15
Christiana Maple (7)	15
Adrian Vuylsteke (7)	16
Lydia Salmon (8)	16
Benjamin Thompson (7)	17
Ana Brace (7)	17
Ally Henderson (11)	18
Jack Bywater (7)	18
Francesca George (10)	19
Kia Henson (10)	19
Ethan Moss (10)	20
Christina Day (10)	21
Joe Pengelly (10)	22
Annie Avery (9)	22
Tom Dixon (10)	23
Lydia Blume (9)	23
Gemma Payton (10)	24
Matthew Carpenter (10)	25
Joshua Peacock (9)	26
Meredith Ash (9)	27
Luke Bucklow (11)	28
Ben Salmon (10)	29
James Green (10)	30
Robyn Barlow (10)	30
Rachel Crosby (11)	31
Jade Reedman (10)	31
Eleanor Sibley (8)	32
Bryony Baker (7)	32
Tom Carter (8)	33
Lewis Irons (7)	33
Reece Turner (8)	34
Jordan Picking (8)	34
Danny Darbyshire (8)	34
Amelia Breacker (7)	35
Georgia Pennell (7)	35
Matthew Davenport (7)	35
Kieran Rouse (8)	36
Georgina Ransome-Jones (8)	36
Hugh Suffield (7)	36
Rory Mooney (7)	37
Joseph Turner (7)	37

Aimee Griffin (8)	53
Georgia Kendall (8)	54

Old Fletton Primary School
Keira Nicholl (10)	54
Chris Goodrum (10)	55
Karl Broughton (10) & Ben George (9)	55
Shannon Murtagh (9)	56
Katie Hibbins (10)	56
Daniella Hodge (9)	56
Jade Frisby (9)	57
Kieran Read (9)	57
Bethany Schofield (9)	57
Konnor Greenhow (10)	58
Sophie Holman (10)	58
Eleanor McMullon (10)	58
Olivia Taylor (9)	59
Lewis Trundell (10)	59
Jordan Turner (10)	59
Lauren Thorndyke (9)	60
Aimee Rotundi (10)	60
Albert Johnson (9)	60
Adam Canham (10)	61
Craig Sayer (9)	61
Safia Djaballah (9)	61

Parnwell Primary School
Shannon Papworth	62
Benjamin Quigley (10)	62
Luke Sharpe	62
Hayley Lawrence (11)	63
Ashley Clarke (11)	63
Jacquelyn Carlton (11)	63
Fiona King (11)	64
Claire Ravenhill (11)	64
Alex Wright (10)	64
Amy Gilbert (11)	65
David Toon (11)	65
Holly Gallacher (11)	66
Kierran Porter	66
Alfie Smith	66

Bernadette Wysockyj 66
Dorinda Vosloo (8) 67
Jacqueline Jones (7) 67
Kayleigh Daulton (10) 67
Rachael Smith (10) 67
Kirstie Denton 68
Connor Jones (8) 68
Rebecca Smith (8) 68
Rebecca Blackledge (10) 69
Amy Wright (10) 69
Luke Oorloff & Dalton Leedell (9) 69
Lauren Clark (9) 69

Perse Preparatory School

Jan Zamirski (10) 70
Dominic Barrett (8) 70
Matthew Evans (9) 71
George Davies (9) 71
Priyan Davda (9) 72
Harry Claydon (9) 72
Fergus Waugh (9) 73
Joshua Walker (9) 73
Toby Phillips (10) 74
William Thwaites (10) 74
Jonathan Heybrock (9) 75
Ollie McLellan (10) 75
Tom O'Keefe (10) 76
Oliver Linehan (9) 76
Huw Oliver (10) 77
Alan Kanapin (9) 77
Alec Jenkins (10) 78
Joe Harper (10) 78
Ben Murray (7) 79
Alex Fanourakis (10) 79
James Cockain (8) 80
Bartu Atamert (7) 80
Ethan Abraham (8) 81
Tom Harwood (8) 81
Nihal Chadha (8) 82
Chris Pepper (8) 82
Leo Bridger (8) 83

Alex Gilbertson (8)	83
Alexander Wilfert (8)	84
Akbar Akhter (8)	84
Ben Winfield (7)	85
David Y C Lau (7)	85
Dominic Strandmann (8)	86
Conor Sullivan (7)	86
Henry Gregory (8)	87
Alex Mitchell (7)	87
Hugh O'Keefe (8)	88
Hugh Goddard (7)	88
Owen Good (8)	89
Mycroft Majumdar (8)	89
Mohammed Zia (8)	90
Thomas Poskitt (8)	90
Edward Chadwick (8)	91
Christopher Stone (8)	91
Jonathan Marrow (8)	92
Remin Harji (7)	92

Queen Edith Community Primary School

Erica Davletov (10)	93
Alice Gooch (10)	93
Cordelia Chui (9)	94
Rishi Verma (9)	94

Walton Junior School

Thomas Rice (7)	95
Sam-Luca Rolph (7)	95
Olivia Margaret Hogan (8)	96
Joshua Saville (7)	96
Megan Somers (8)	97
Joshua Hales (7)	97
Glen Thompson (7)	98
Georgia Armfield (8)	98
Noah Bell (8)	98
Asha Green (7)	99
Amy Allen (8)	99
Charlotte Griffin (8)	99
Sabrina Giordano (7)	100
Holly Kaminski (7)	100

Tanisha Speechley (7)	101
Joseph Smith (7)	101
Eleanor Jones (7)	102
Daisy Bews (7)	102
Adam Rooney (8)	102
Chloe Griffin (8)	103
Ashlie Coward (8)	104

Wilburton VPC School

Bethany Flack (9)	104
Hayden Coe (10)	105
Katie Easton (9)	106
Georgia-May Baylis (10)	107
Coral Gilbert (10)	108
Ross Payne (9)	109
Jennifer Weldon (10)	110
Mellissa Binks (10)	111
Anjela Griffiths (10)	112
Josh Greene (9)	113
Harley Pyne (9)	114
Philip Kirby (9)	115

Winhills County Primary School

Stacey Lee George (9)	115
Ayeshia Evans (9)	116
Sam Everett (8)	116
Peter Housden (7)	116
Jack Hayward (7)	117
Josh Hattle (11)	117
Vanessa Aveling (10)	117
Dale Banim (10)	118
Ryan Whittingham (11)	118
Lauren Daye (11)	118
Bobby Hubbard (10)	119
Jonathan Huggett (10)	119
Matthew Beckett (10)	119
Tiana Fabray-Smith (8)	120
David Maddy (11)	120
Timothy Franklin (10)	121
Hayley Curtis (10)	121
Kirsty Carter (9)	122

Wittering Primary School

The Poems

Answering Service

If you want to find the man who made this answering service
And shoot him with a gun . . .
Press 1
If you want to find the man who made this answering service
And pelt him with poo . . .
Press 2
If you want to find the man who made this answering service
And hit him with a tree . . .
Press 3
If you want to find the man who made this answering service
And feed him to a boar . . .
Press 4
If you want to find the man who made this answering service
And smother his face with chives . . .
Press 5
If you want to find the man who made this answering service
And throw at him sticks . . .
Press 6
If you want to find the man who made this answering service
And ban him from Devon . . .
Press 7
If you want to find the man who made this answering service
And whack him with slate . . .
Press 8
If you want to find the man who made this answering service
And throw him into a mine . . .
Press 9.

Ryan Markley (10)

Winter Haiku

Snow is on the ground
Gloves and scarves are very wet
It is cold outside.

Jessica Garrison (11)
Brington CE Primary School

Football

F ootball is great, football is fun
O h, look at Ronaldo run
O h, look at that skill, oh, look at that skill
T hat goal he just scored was brill
B rilliant play, look at him go
A great goal, look at him go
L ove Ronaldo getting the entire thrill
L ook at them, they beat them 4-0.

Aron Campbell (9)
Brington CE Primary School

The Fox And The Hunt Haiku

Running through the wood
Jumping through the stream and hedge
Being chased by dogs.

Kiri Saunders (11)
Brington CE Primary School

Colours Haiku

Red, yellow, pink, green
All the colours I have seen
The rainbow colours.

Eloise Scott (10)
Brington CE Primary School

Water Fights Haiku

I love water fights
Here comes the hosepipe, oh no!
Here it comes *aargh! Splash!*

Liam Robinson (10)
Brington CE Primary School

Dark, Dark
(Based on the book 'Funny Bones' by Janet and Allan Ahlberg)

In a dark, dark wood,
There was a dark, dark house,
In the dark, dark house, there was a dark, dark room,
In the dark, dark room, there was a dark, dark cupboard,
In the dark, dark cupboard, there was a dark, dark drawer,
In the dark, dark drawer, there was a . . .
Ghost!

Thomas Burrows Smith (9)
Brington CE Primary School

Time

Time goes fast, faster than lightning
When it goes past, it's frightening
Time goes fast when you are in bed
Thoughts spinning round inside my head.

Philip Mannis (9)
Brington CE Primary School

Playtime Haiku

All running outside
Getting your hats, coats and scarves
You must not be last.

Amelia Cobley (10)
Brington CE Primary School

My Lovely Bed Haiku

I get in my bed
It is really cosy and warm
Oh no! It's morning!

George Fleming (10)
Brington CE Primary School

My Family

Mummy, Mummy, she's always in a hurry to go to work.
Daddy, Daddy, never gets up to go to the building site.
Mummy, Mummy, she is really lazy at night.
Daddy, Daddy, is really fun and cool.
Mummy, Mummy, is really fun sometimes.
Daddy, Daddy, always comes back late.

Harry Girvan (7)
Brington CE Primary School

My Family

Daddy, Daddy, gets up slowly.
Daddy, Daddy, like a lion.

Mummy, Mummy, gets up quickly.
Mummy, Mummy, is running
Around the house like an ostrich.

Patrick Matthews (8)
Brington CE Primary School

Haiku

Crash! Boom! Crash! Boom! Crash!
There is an elephant, *splat!*
He just sneezed on me.

Colin Fox (10)
Brington CE Primary School

Paperclips Haiku

Paperclips are fun
You can make a thousand things
Paperclips are best.

Robert Allison (10)
Brington CE Primary School

Butterfly

B utterflies have pretty spots
U nderneath they have big, black dots
T heir tentacles are very small
T hey can also be very tall
E very day you shine like glitter
R unning away makes you look so bitter
F lies always get in my way
L ike a horrible, big, black stray
Y ou'd better watch out for butterflies.

Eliza Fleming (8)
Brington CE Primary School

Cats

There are black cats,
Grey cats,
Even little stripy cats.

Ginger cats,
Long whiskered cats
And very big ones too.

Jack Johnson (9)
Brington CE Primary School

My Family

Daddy, Daddy, all curled up in bed.
Daddy, Daddy, too lazy to get up today
Because it is Monday.

Mummy, Mummy, getting up early,
She rushes downstairs
Gobbles down her breakfast
And rushes off to work.

Patrick Brighty (8)
Brington CE Primary School

Cat On A Road Haiku

A cat on the road
I don't think it will get far
It's not in a car.

Jacob Murphy (10)
Brington CE Primary School

The Deep Blue Sea

The sea is warm
The sea is calm
The sea is as smooth
As the skin on your palm.

The sea can flow
The sea can dance
The sea can tap
Like a monkey in a trance.

The sea is rocky
The sea is blue
The sea is louder
Than a cow that says, *'Moo!'*

The sea is so sparkly
The sea, it glistens
And when it is night
It seems like it listens.

The sea is wavy
The sea is whirly
The sea is shimmering
The sea is twirly.

Abby Elizabeth Wright (7)
Buckden CE Primary School

All About The Sea

The sea can swish,
The sea can prance,
The sea can blow,
The sea can dance.

The sea can glide,
The sea can tear,
The sea can roar,
Like an angry bear.

The sea can be calm,
The sea can be rocky,
The sea can be nice,
Like a bear playing hockey.

The sea can flow,
The sea can tow,
The sea can blow
Like an angry buffalo.

Oliver Bailey (7)
Buckden CE Primary School

The Locomotion Sea

The sea is rocky
The sea is tough
The sea is scary
Like a bear that is rough.

The sea is smooth
The sea is soft
The sea is lovely
Like a gentle moth.

George Haverson (7)
Buckden CE Primary School

The Sea

The sea can be rocky
The sea can be wavy
The sea is salty
The sea is lazy.

The sea can be steady
The sea can doze
The sea can sneeze
Like a giant's nose.

The sea can be strong
The sea can be choppy
The sea can be wishy
The sea can be sloppy.

Imogen Herdman (8)
Buckden CE Primary School

The Sea

The sea can jump
The sea can be rough
The sea can be crazy
The sea can be tough.

The sea can roll
The sea can be silly
The sea can be strong
Like a frog on a lily.

The sea can be quiet
The sea can be loud
The sea can be calm
Like a big, grey cloud.

April Carter (7)
Buckden CE Primary School

A Sunny Day With The Sea

The sea is gentle
The sea is calm
The sea is soft
Like it's crawling on your palm.

The sea can be warm
The sea can be alive
The sea can be loud
Like a crazy beehive.

The sea is salty
The sea is sandy
When you want to sail
The sea can be handy.

Olivia Sienna Haverson (7)
Buckden CE Primary School

A Sunny Day With The Sea

The sea is gentle
The sea is alive
The sea is loud
The sea is like a big beehive.

The sea can sway
The sea can swish
The sea can prance
Like a hungry fish.

The sea can splosh
The sea is crazy
The sea can whisper
The sea can be lazy.

Harriet Frost (8)
Buckden CE Primary School

The Sea

The sea is calm
The sea is pale
The sea is crawling
Like a small, grey snail.

The sea can be stormy
The sea can be grand
The sea can be a bully
To the grains of dry sand.

The sea can be wavy
The sea can run
The sea can be nice
And ready for fun.

The sea can call grey clouds
The sea can call rain
The sea can call lightning
And it's a stormy night again.

Madelen Shepherd (7)
Buckden CE Primary School

The Sea

The sea can be loud
The sea can be rough
The sea can be gentle
The sea can be tough.

The sea can be alive
The sea can be rocky
The sea can be wavy
The sea can be choppy.

The sea can be strong
The sea can be lazy
The sea can be salty
The sea can be crazy.

Abbey Furmedge (7)
Buckden CE Primary School

The Deep Blue Sea

The sea is warm
The sea is calm
The sea is as smooth
As the skin on your palm.

The sea can flow
The sea can blow
And when it gets angry
It knows how to go.

The sea can get giant
The sea can get tough
The sea makes an earthquake
If it tries hard enough.

Ana Nash (8)
Buckden CE Primary School

The Sea Can Be . . .

The sea can be scary
The sea can bash
The sea can be nasty
The sea can smash.

The sea can be angry
The sea can be rough
The sea can blow
The sea can be tough.

The sea is warm
The sea is calm
The sea is as smooth
As your mother's palm.

Oliver Simpson (7)
Buckden CE Primary School

The Sea Song

The sea is high
The sea can fly
It's a blur
Like a bat going by.

The sea can be bad
The sea can be tough
The sea can be mad
Like a bear that's rough.

The sea can be calm
The sea can be nice
The sea can flow
Like mice on ice.

The sea can be wild
The sea can be crazy
The sea can call whirlpools
Like a bear that's not lazy.

Sam Crane (8)
Buckden CE Primary School

The Sea

The sea can jump
The sea can be rough
The sea can be crazy
The sea can be tough
Like a loud, little dog.

The sea can be strong
The sea can be loud
The sea is alive
Like a big, crazy crowd.

The sea can be calm
The sea can be slow
The sea is quiet
Like a sleeping crow.

Kira Blume (7)
Buckden CE Primary School

Counting Rhyme

One by one
One by one
Children singing
In the sun.

Two by two
Two by two
Would you like
To join them too?

Three by three
Three by three
Children splashing
In the sea.

Dasho Atkin (8)
Buckden CE Primary School

The Sea

The sea can be soft
The sea can be smooth
The sea can be calm
And the sea can soothe.

The sea can be bad
The sea can be cold
The sea can be wonderful
Like a pot of gold.

The sea can be high
The sea can be steady
The sea can be slow
As a falling teddy.

Shelby Pell (7)
Buckden CE Primary School

The Sea

The sea can be scary
The sea can tow
The sea can go
Like a huge buffalo.

The sea can be strange
The sea can be freaky
The sea can be cheeky
The sea can be sneaky.

The sea can be big
The sea can be tough
The sea can be gloomy
The sea can be rough.

Sam Hitchin (8)
Buckden CE Primary School

The Sea

The sea can be gentle
The sea can be glistening
The sea can be quiet
The sea is whispering.

The sea can be blue
The sea can be bright
The sea can be warm
Like a summer's night.

The sea can be wavy
The sea can be swirling
The sea can be graceful
Like a ballerina twirling.

Joseph Bradley (8)
Buckden CE Primary School

The Sea

The sea is salty
The sea is calm
The sea is enchanting
Like a charm.

The sea is rough
The sea is choppy
The sea is tough
And sometimes happy.

The sea can be sploshy
The sea can be crazy
The sea can be loud
The sea can be wavy.

Scarlett Andrews (7)
Buckden CE Primary School

The Sea

The sea is strong
The sea is wavy
The sea is rocky
The sea is crazy.

The sea can whisper
The sea can roll
The sea can flow
Like a creeping mole.

The sea can chop
The sea can snap
The sea can boom
Like a giant clap.

Christiana Maple (7)
Buckden CE Primary School

The Sea

The sea can be glistening
The sea can be shining
The sea can be lovely
The sea can be gliding.

The sea can do whispers
The sea can be wavy
The sea can be flowing
Like a bucket of gravy.

The sea can be rough
The sea can be alive
The sea can be choppy
Like a busy beehive.

The sea likes to be tough
The sea can be crashing
The sea can be jumping
The sea likes to be thrashing.

Adrian Vuylsteke (7)
Buckden CE Primary School

The Summer Sea

The sun is out
The sea is glowing
The sea is salty
The sea is flowing.

The sea is wild
The sea goes *boo*
The sea is jumpy
Like a kangaroo.

The sea is rocky
The sea is a log
The sea is crazy
Like a barking dog.

Lydia Salmon (8)
Buckden CE Primary School

The Sea

The sea can swish
The sea can be bright
The sea can soothe
Like a summer's night.

The sea can go wild
The sea can tow
The sea can tear
Like a big buffalo.

The sea can crash
The sea can dance
The sea can move
Like a man in a trance.

Benjamin Thompson (7)
Buckden CE Primary School

The Sea

The sea can be strong
The sea can be bad
The sea can cry
Like a tiger that is sad.

The sea can be blue
The sea can be rough
The sea can be loud
The sea can be tough.

The sea can be rocky
The sea can be swirly
The sea can be wishy
And sometimes whirly.

Ana Brace (7)
Buckden CE Primary School

The Contents Of The Cauldron

Double, double, toil and trouble,
Cooking pot stir up some trouble.

Eye of a newt, leg of a toad,
Bladder of bat, a bald man's cold.

Essence of smallpox, ear of a cat,
Tail of an ox, wing of a gnat.

Venom of viper, sting of a wasp,
Heart of a quail, brain of the best.

Teacher of physics, to go with a snake,
Grandpa Simpson, boil and bake.

Double, double, toil and trouble,
Cooking pot stir up some trouble.

PC Mac, an iPod too,
Smashed together, in a shoe.

An Everton scarf, covered in barf,
The Liverpool team, oh, supreme!

Ally Henderson (11)
Buckden CE Primary School

The Sea Can Be

The sea can be loud
The sea can tear
The sea can be selfish
Like a hungry bear.

The sea can be quiet
The sea can stroke
The sea can be kind
But can sometimes choke.

Jack Bywater (7)
Buckden CE Primary School

The Witches' Spell

Red-hot spice
Blood of mice
Snake venom
Purple denim.

Cow's tongue
A human lung
Bull's horn
Magic unicorn.

Human fat
Slice of bat
A long toenail
A fluffy dog tail.

Double, double, toil and trouble
Fire burn and cauldron bubble!

Francesca George (10)
Buckden CE Primary School

The Witches' Cauldron Poem

Double, double, toil and trouble,
Fire burns and cauldron's bubble.
Into the cauldron where the humans bubble,
Round and round, where the rats go down.
Sneaking hamsters, just like witches' laughter!
Double, double, toil and trouble,
Fire burns and cauldron's bubble.
Eye of frog, toe of dog in a fish's fin,
Tail of dog and leg of hog, lizards, worms,
Burn, burn, burn!

Kia Henson (10)
Buckden CE Primary School

Witches' Poem

Blood of a mime,
Eye of a fighter of crime,
Alligator spice
And blood of mice.

Double, double
I've seen trouble,
Fire burn and cauldron bubble.

Blood of a fool,
Make this man cool,
Brown soil,
Blood-stained foil.

Double, double,
I've seen trouble,
Fire burn and cauldron bubble.

Snake skin
And dolphin fin,
Feather of a golden eagle,
Head of a seagull.

Double, double,
I've seen trouble,
Fire burn and cauldron bubble.

Human flubber,
Piece of white rubber,
Chelsea player,
Wrapped in a map full of fat.

Double, double,
I've seen trouble,
Fire burn and cauldron bubble.

A head of a rat,
Man U's shirt full of fat,
Raven's eye,
Fall off a cliff, goodbye.

Double, double,
I've seen trouble,
Fire burn and cauldron bubble.

Ethan Moss (10)
Buckden CE Primary School

The Witches Prepare Their Cauldron

Keep on boiling poisonous spell,
What will it do? No one can tell.

First, in goes the long, worm's slime,
Leave it boiling till five minutes time.
Then you add the spider's legs,
All mashed up with washing line pegs.

Keep on boiling poisonous spell,
What will it do? No one can tell.

Next, in goes a human eye,
That will make our victim cry.
You will need a pussy cat's tail
And a tiger's fingernail.

Keep on boiling poisonous spell,
What will it do? No one can tell.

Christina Day (10)
Buckden CE Primary School

The Witches' Spell

Double, double, toilet bubble
Cooking pot let's stir up trouble
In my cooking pot I'll put
Extremely smelly mouse foot.

Ear of a mouse
A blown-up house.

Big, fat bull, scared squirrel
Foot of a toad will make you shrivel.

Homework book and eye of a bug
Croak of a frog, slime of a slug.

Dead old donkey and a cat
Will make a nice, toasted bat.

A mucky shoe, fin of a shark
This dog will soon have no bark.

A stinky duck covered in muck
A big chicken with no cluck.

Joe Pengelly (10)
Buckden CE Primary School

Nonsense Poem

There was once a small, little mouse
He lived in a Jaffa Cake house,
He knew a massive, big bunny,
The bunny thought he was funny,
The bunny lived in a box,
Until he moved in with a fox,
The fox ate the bunny,
The mouse thought it was funny.

Annie Avery (9)
Buckden CE Primary School

Witch Poem

Two fat cats and one big dog
One big rabbit and a bowl of frogs.

Hubba bubba, eat your flubba,
Turn my spell into glubba.

Two pig ears we would know
Ten eyeballs, in they go.

Hubba bubba, eat your flubba,
Turn my spell into glubba.

Two bat wings and a gallon of blood,
Just enough to have a bud.

Hubba bubba, eat your flubba,
Turn my spell into glubba.

Tom Dixon (10)
Buckden CE Primary School

The Witches' Cauldron Poem

Double, double, toil and trouble,
Fire burn and cauldron bubble.
Fillet of a flickering snake,
In the cauldron, boil and bake.
One hairy, old pig's germ,
One fat, slimy worm.
Next, the head of a fish,
It will make a nice dish.
Then a shark's tail,
Mixed with the head of a male.
Lizard's tail, a dog's tooth,
All we need is a little *poof!*

Lydia Blume (9)
Buckden CE Primary School

A Witch's Cauldron Poem

Double, double,
Toil and trouble,
Fire burn
And cauldron bubble.

A cup full of poison,
A head of a snake,
Which will be the bait.
Day and night,
There'll be bait.

Double, double,
Toil and trouble,
Fire burn
And cauldron bubble.

A teacher's bag,
With a coffee stain,
This will be quite lame.

Double, double,
Toil and trouble,
Fire burn
And cauldron bubble.

A classroom's mess
And a snake's silly hiss,
A friend's piece of hair,
This is a pair,
Your little stair,
Will be a dare.

Double, double,
Toil and trouble,
Fire burn
And cauldron bubble.

Gemma Payton (10)
Buckden CE Primary School

Witches' Spell Poem

Round the cauldron we can go,
Two venomous snake fangs, in they go,
Spleen of pig,
Foot of juicy fig,
Slime of slug,
Salt shark fin,
Eyeball of cat,
They are fat.

Double, double, toil and trouble,
Fire burn and cauldron bubble,
Ink of seahorse,
Stomach of octopus,
Gut of wombat,
Head of mouse,
Blood of wolf,
Tongue of whale,
Scale of dragon.

Double, double, toil and trouble,
Fire burn and cauldron bubble,
Body of newt,
Fur of tiger,
Baby bat,
Bird wing,
The feathers of an ostrich,
Skin of worm,
Tail of horse.

Double, double, toil and trouble,
Fire burn and cauldron bubble.

Matthew Carpenter (10)
Buckden CE Primary School

Witches' Cauldron Poem

Double, double, toil and trouble,
Fire burn and cauldron bubble,
Even though we like cow skin,
Oh, my favourite's a rapper in a bin.

I put in a hairy dog's tail,
Yes, another person's fingernail.

Double, double, toil and trouble,
Fire burn and cauldron bubble,
Now you need an eye of a fish,
Then you need to smash a dish.

Get a really big person's eye,
But if you don't, you would die.

Double, double, toil and trouble,
Fire burn and cauldron bubble,
Always get an old person's heart,
Then get an old, mouldy tart.

After that, get a really big fly,
After that, a smelly old pie.

Double, double, toil and trouble,
Fire burn and cauldron bubble,
If you get a sharp shark's tooth,
Oh no, the shark will go *poof!*

Joshua Peacock (9)
Buckden CE Primary School

The Witches' Spell

Double, double, toil and trouble,
Fire burn and cauldron bubble.

Monkey's spine
Blood wine!

Crocodile's spice
And eyes of mice.

Spider's leg
And toad's head.

Double, double, toil and trouble,
Fire burn and cauldron bubble.

Bat's lung
And hawk's tongue.

Bull's horn
A cow's newborn.

Into cauldron blood goes round,
Down, down the snake's head goes.

Wasp's sting
Pigeon's wing.

Dog's ear
And blood-sucking fears!

Double, double, toil and trouble,
Fire burn and cauldron bubble.

Meredith Ash (9)
Buckden CE Primary School

Sounds At A Football Match

Tuesday night
When it was not light,
I went to a football match at Upton Park
And I gave West Ham a top mark.

Teenagers shouting, 'Foul!'
And somewhere on the pitch I could hear an, *'Ow!'*
Adults breaking the important rule,
No bad language at all!

When Etherington scored a goal,
The crowd went ballistic and couldn't believe it at all.
Rotherham's goalie kicked the ball,
But a Rotherham player had a nasty fall.

The free kick was not good,
Not as good as West Ham could!
The referee's whistle went off at half-time,
It was time to get a lemon and lime.

Rotherham were down and couldn't get up,
If they wanted to get up, they needed to hurry.
Oh no! Five minutes to go!

Time is up,
They're going down,
But now the crowd are singing,
'I'm forever blowing bubbles!'

Luke Bucklow (11)
Buckden CE Primary School

Witches' Spell Poem

Round the cauldron we will go,
Three cats' eyeballs, in they go,
Slime of a slug's liver in,
As we add more bugs for me,
Double, double, toil and trouble,
Fire burn and cauldron bubble,
The fangs of a rat,
The gut of a bat,
Teeth of a shark,
Blood of a wolf,
The head of a dwarf,
The tongue of a whale,
That looked quite pale,
Fur of a lion,
Double, double, toil and trouble,
Fire burn and cauldron bubble,
A wing of a bird,
The tail of a horse,
The nose of a pig,
With a great big fig,
The lung of a tiger,
An eyebrow of a cheetah,
Double, double, toil and trouble,
Fire burn and cauldron bubble.

Ben Salmon (10)
Buckden CE Primary School

The Witches' Cauldron Poem

First, the head of a dead fish
It will make a lovely dish.

Then, you'll need the eye of a frog
And the giant tooth of a wild hog.

Double, double, toil and trouble,
Fire burn and cauldron bubble.

An eaten rat from a snake,
In the oven, boil and bake.

Then you get some hair from the mayor
And a tooth from a football player.

Double, double, toil and trouble,
Fire burn and cauldron bubble.

James Green (10)
Buckden CE Primary School

The Witches' Cauldron

Double, double, toil and trouble,
Fire burning, cauldron bubble.

One tail from a dog,
One head from a frog.
A bumble bee's sting
And a hairy bat's wing.

Double, double, toil and trouble,
Fire burning, cauldron bubble.

One shell of a snail,
Ten bits of dirty nail.
Five bits of snake's insides,
While other creatures run and hide!

Robyn Barlow (10)
Buckden CE Primary School

The Seaside Sounds

I went to the seaside one day
And I will tell you what I heard.
The sound of the children chattering
And a screeching bird.

The shouting of the swimmers,
The tinkling ice cream truck,
The splashing of the waves
And a lolly for you to suck.

The laughing of the people,
On the squeaking, funfair rides,
Other people screaming,
Don't fall out the sides.

The sound of braying donkeys,
The laughing of the clowns,
The clapping at the puppet show,
Oh! no one ever frowns.

Rachel Crosby (11)
Buckden CE Primary School

The Witches' Cauldron Poem

Double, double, toil and trouble,
Fire burn and cauldron bubble.
Round, round, get the rats down,
Jumping snail, just like a clown.
Rats, rats, we love rats,
Put them in with the cats.
Double, double, toil and trouble,
Fire burn and cauldron bubble.

Jade Reedman (10)
Buckden CE Primary School

The Sea

The sea can *spit*
The sea can *bubble*
The sea can *rule*
Like I'm in *trouble.*

The sea can be *fat*
The sea can *cuddle*
The sea can *fall*
Like I'm in a *muddle.*

The sea can *shout*
The sea can be *bad*
The sea can *growl*
Like my angry *dad!*

Eleanor Sibley (8)
Buckden CE Primary School

The Sea

The sea can growl
The sea can howl
The sea can rip
Like an angry owl.

The sea can tear
The sea can hail
The sea can jump
Like a baby whale.

The sea can rock
The sea can scream
The sea can rip
Like a football team.

Bryony Baker (7)
Buckden CE Primary School

The Sea

The sea can smash
The sea can be tall
The sea can crash
As the waves fall.

The sea can be choppy
The sea can pounce
The sea can come in
Like a dog that can bounce.

The sea can be kind
The sea can be flat
The sea can be gentle
Like a mouse who is fat.

Tom Carter (8)
Buckden CE Primary School

The Sea

The sea can growl
The sea can strand
The sea can spark
Like a noisy band.

The sea can drown
The sea can wash
The sea can sweep
Like a super *splosh!*

The sea can growl
The sea can wail
The sea can speed
Like the earthquake hail.

Lewis Irons (7)
Buckden CE Primary School

The Sea

The sea can growl
The sea can spark
The sea can be wild
Like a lion in the dark.

The sea can strand
The sea can wash
The sea can sweep
With a giant *splosh!*

Reece Turner (8)
Buckden CE Primary School

The Sea

The sea can growl
The sea can hail
The sea can wail
Like a baby quail.

The sea can howl
The sea can rip
The sea can tear
Like a big tip.

Jordan Picking (8)
Buckden CE Primary School

The Sea

The sea can scream
The sea can growl
The sea can cry
Like a dog that howls.

The sea is big
The sea is small
The sea is quiet
Like a beach ball.

Danny Darbyshire (8)
Buckden CE Primary School

The Sea

The sea can spit
The sea can tear
The sea can rip
Like a giant bear.

The sea can shout
The sea can roar
The sea can be quiet
Like a bear who wants more.

The sea can be rough
The sea can be calm
The sea can be hot
Like a giant charm.

Amelia Breacker (7)
Buckden CE Primary School

The Sea

The sea can be angry
The sea can be proud
The sea can be cross
Like a scruffy cloud.

The sea can be rough
The sea can splash
The sea can be big
Like the sound of a bash.

Georgia Pennell (7)
Buckden CE Primary School

The Sea

The sea can be mental
The sea can be flat
The sea can be wavy
Like a big mat.

Matthew Davenport (7)
Buckden CE Primary School

The Sea

The sea can snarl
The sea can growl
The sea can crash
Like a wolf's howl.

The sea can wail
The sea can scream
The sea can thump
Like a bad dream.

Kieran Rouse (8)
Buckden CE Primary School

The Sea

The sea can be angry
The sea can be proud
The sea can be mysterious
Like a thunder cloud.

The sea can be wavy
The sea can be big
The sea can be horrid
Like a screaming pig.

Georgina Ransome-Jones (8)
Buckden CE Primary School

The Sea

The sea can burn
Like a toaster.
The sea can swirl
Like a roller coaster.

The sea can howl
Like a dog.
The sea can tumble
Like a falling log.

Hugh Suffield (7)
Buckden CE Primary School

The Sea

The sea can growl
The sea can rip
The sea can scream
Like a swinging whip.

The sea can be calm
The sea can be flat
The sea can be soft
Like a sleeping cat.

Rory Mooney (7)
Buckden CE Primary School

The Sea

The sea can be mean
The sea can be trying
The sea can be cross
Like I am when I'm crying.

The sea can be happy
The sea can be flat
The sea can be quiet
Like a sleeping cat.

Joseph Turner (7)
Buckden CE Primary School

The Sea

The sea can rule
The sea can spit
The sea can be tall
Like a hand that hits.

The sea can damage
The sea can be mean
The sea can be choppy
Like a huge, long stream.

Charlotte Turnbull (7)
Buckden CE Primary School

Buckden Counting Rhyme

One by one
One by one
Children playing
In the sun.

Two by two
Two by two
Children's jumpers
Red and blue.

Three by three
Three by three
Children playing
With cut knees.

Four by four
Four by four
Everyone sitting
On the floor.

Callum Leach (7)
Buckden CE Primary School

The Sea

The sea can howl
The sea can bash
The sea can get stronger
Like a plate going *smash!*

The sea can calm down
The sea can get choppy
The sea can slow down
Like seaweed that's sloppy.

The sea can be fast
The sea can be rough
The sea can be high
Like it's big and tough.

Robert Bond (7)
Buckden CE Primary School

The Sea

The sea can be loud
The sea can be proud
The sea can be horrible
Like a scraggy cloud.

The sea can be roaring
The sea can be loud
The sea can be vicious
Like a great big crowd.

The sea can be naughty
The sea can be flat
The sea can be stupid
Like a great big prat.

Amelia Dean (8)
Buckden CE Primary School

The Sea

The sea can be big
The sea can be cool
The sea can be swirly
Like a big whirlpool.

The sea can be cold
The sea can be hot
The sea can be choppy
Like a bubbly pot.

The sea can be loud
The sea can be small
The sea can be scary
Like a horrible school.

Lucy Bowden (8)
Buckden CE Primary School

The Sea

The sea can growl
The sea can thump
The sea can scream
Like a crashing bump.

The sea can scream
The sea can crash
The sea can growl
Like a big bash.

Joseph Thomas (7)
Buckden CE Primary School

The Sea

The sea can growl
The sea can bash
The sea can howl
Like a car crash.

The sea can growl
The sea can scream
The sea can howl
Like a bad dream.

Elliot O'Driscoll (7)
Buckden CE Primary School

The Sea

The sea can growl
The sea can tear
The sea can splash
Like a bossy bear.

The sea can growl
The sea can wail
The sea can hail
Like a baby quail.

Catherine Graves (7)
Buckden CE Primary School

Willow Chant

Round about the willow go
In the nagging teachers throw
Do it slowly, bit by bit
Throw them viciously in the pit
In go pens and reading books
Pots and pans and all the cooks
Willow, willow, rule the school
Mixing up the thick, green gruel.

In the chalk and blackboards go
As others look for things to throw
Keep the snails, they are cool
They can help us rule the school
Keep the climbing apparatus
Do not try to separate us
Willow, willow, rule the school
Mixing up the thick, green gruel
Then we really are cool.

Shaun Prince (10) & John Clark (11)
Great Staughton Primary School

Willow Potion

Hour by hour,
The potion gains power,
The cauldron simmers,
The blue liquid glimmers.
In go the books,
Teachers and cooks,
In go the chairs,
A kid stands and stares,
In he goes for now he knows
That the potion has been made.

James Robins-Johnson (11)
Great Staughton Primary School

Willow Chant

Round the willow go,
In the nagging teachers throw,
Do it slowly, bit by bit,
Throw them viciously in the pit,
In go pens and reading books,
Pots, pans and all the cooks,
Willow, willow, rule the school,
Mixing up the thick, green gruel.

Throw in desks and smash the chairs,
Rip apart the class teddy bears,
Pit is boiling, too hot to risk,
In goes chalk and floppy disks,
School whistle, bells and booster books,
Rip the homework books and cooks,
Willow, willow, rule the school,
Mixing up the thick, green gruel.

In go the chalky boards
And smashing windows with the doors,
In go speakers and the lot,
Get rid of Chestnut's old, manky cot,
Mixing beech, hazel too,
A bit of rowan will have to do,
Get the snails and the pot,
Crush them up, kill the lot,
Willow, willow, rule the school,
Mixing up the thick, green gruel.

Hattie Morton (10)
Great Staughton Primary School

Bang! - Haiku

He came through the trees
The deer could eat in peace now
The bullet went *bang!*

April Mullings (11)
Great Staughton Primary School

Willow Chant

(Inspired by Act IV, Scene I of 'Macbeth' by William Shakespeare)

In and out the willow tree
Nagging teachers, one, two, three
In the cauldron they all twirl
Mix them up really well
In go pens and reading books
In go ones with nasty looks
Willow, willow, rule the school
Mixing up the thick, green gruel.

In and out the dinner room
Dinner ladies shout and zoom
Pots and pans will start to smell
If they don't wash them really well
Willow, willow, rule the school
Mixing up the thick, green gruel.

Robert Clark (11)
Great Staughton Primary School

Amazing Fruit

Crunchy carrots, orange and raw
When I eat them, they hurt my jaw.

Amazing apples, good to eat
Amazingly, they are so sweet.

Singing sweetcorn, small and round
When you eat them, they make a sound.

Bouncing bananas, long and thin
When you eat them, they touch your chin.

Greg Thorndick (10)
Great Staughton Primary School

Goodbye School

Round about the cauldron go,
In the nagging teachers throw.
Hit them hard with a sticky Pritt stick,
If that's not enough, then give them a kick.
Throw in all the books and pens,
Finally, school has met its end.

Double, double, toil and trouble,
Teachers burn and school work bubbles.

Throw in all the art supplies,
I think it's time to say goodbyes.
Before you go, add homework books
And all the kids with scary looks.
Mash them up until they yell,
Now they're under the children's spell.

Double, double, toil and trouble,
Teachers burn and school work bubbles.

Ellie Nethaway (11)
Great Staughton Primary School

Chocolate Dream

When I eat sweeties, it makes me *think!*
Of all the people in leisure centres and gyms, trying to be a . . .
Smaller size, when here I am eating succulent, chocolate
And feeling *sweet!*
Chocolate, choc-o-late cream!
It's all so tasty, you have to dream!
Eat it and it tastes *extreme!*
Chocolate!

Rebecca Wilkinson (11)
Great Staughton Primary School

Willow Chant

Round about the willow go,
In the nagging teachers throw,
Do it slowly, bit by bit,
Throw them viciously in the pit.
In go pens and reading books,
Pots and pans and all the cooks.

Put in all the table grids
And cruelly torture the naughty kids.
If they love school, then they're not cool
And chuck them in with all the gruel.
Mix it quick and shut the lid
And feed it to Headmaster Sid!

Potions, potions, they will glow,
Drink them up and out they go!

Toby Darlow & Sam Amos (10)
Great Staughton Primary School

Healthy Living

Scrub your body,
Nice and clean,
Brush your teeth,
Until they gleam!

Pearly whites,
Smelling sweet,
No smelly breath,
No smelly feet!

Clean and healthy,
Top to toe,
Healthy living,
Here we go!

Connie Owens (11)
Great Staughton Primary School

My School

It was a hot, summer's day,
The school was lovely, pretty,
There was a little wind
Hitting the windows soft, smooth.

The summer's day turned hotter,
The day turned brighter.

The children were in the pool,
The water looked like shiny glass,
The water was cool,
The water was that shiny, it blinded me.

The summer's day turned hotter,
The day turned brighter.

The rooms are beautiful,
The rooms are light,
The rooms are decorated,
The rooms are heated.

The summer's day turned hotter,
The day turned brighter.

Paige Johnston (8)
Gunthorpe Primary School

Tree

The tree gets more legendary as it grows,
The tree will still stand in 50 years,
The leaves sway, like flags in the wind,
The tree is as tall as a giraffe,
The tree is as brown as a bear,
The tree is as wrinkled as a grandma.

Jay Modhvadia (8)
Gunthorpe Primary School

A Noisy, Cold Day

As I walked through Gunthorpe that day
People going past me said, 'Oh my word, I must say!'
The cold wind on my face
With Dad behind me, I made myself quicken the pace.

Cars whizzing here and there
People screeching in the air
And as I passed Gunthorpe School, I could hardly believe the racket
And this I might put in brackets.

And so our journey comes to an end
There is me, huddled with my friends
As we walk down the street
We worry about our sore feet.

Abbie Brooks (9)
Gunthorpe Primary School

Features Of A Poem

As I walked past Gunthorpe School
I saw people being friendly to one another
As I walked past the class
They chatted like a radio station.

The tree trunks were as brown as a dog
The uniform was as blue as the sea
The sun was shining bright in the light
The sun was yellow, like gold.

The jumpers were as black as the dark
The chairs were as brown as an owl
The pictures were as colourful as a rainbow.

Deminique Malyon (8)
Gunthorpe Primary School

My Local Area

It was cold as I walked round the school
The wind was pounding on me.
The wind was swishing on me, like a hurricane
As I walked out of the school gate.

Suddenly, the sun came out
It was so bright, it nearly blinded me!
All the flowers popped their heads up and winked at me
They smiled and played games.

The sun is shining!
The sun is shining!

I saw kids splashing in a pool
The water was shining, like the sun
The water was cool.

The sun is shining!
The sun is shining!

Samantha Setchfield (8)
Gunthorpe Primary School

My Best Friend

My best friend is kind and caring
My best friend always plays with me
My best friend always likes to have some fun
My best friend is my number one.

My best friend's hair shines like the sun
My best friend can run, hop and skip
My best friend never gets into trouble at school
My best friend's smile always makes me feel happy.

My best friend wipes away my tears
My best friend makes school so much fun
My best friend's name is Sophie
My best friend is my number one.

Jordan Morley Boom (8)
Gunthorpe Primary School

Gunthorpe School Over The Years

Beginning young and getting old,
Gunthorpe School still stands,
When it was new in 1963,
Builders had dirty hands.

Gunthorpe School in 2005,
Was filled with nature's air,
Being cared for by Mr Ratley,
With loving, caring, care.

Beginning young and getting old,
Gunthorpe School still stands,
When it was new in 1963,
Builders had dirty hands.

Gunthorpe School in 1963,
Next to a small row of houses,
Also next to a farm,
They got a lot of field mice.

Beginning young and getting old,
Gunthorpe School still stands,
When it was new in 1963,
Builders had dirty hands.

Danielle Turner (8)
Gunthorpe Primary School

Pets

Pets, pets, thousands of pets
Rabbits, dogs, cats and fish.
I like pets, all kinds of pets
Nice pets, naughty pets
Small pets, big pets
Clean pets, dirty pets
Smelly pets, not smelly pets.
Pets, pets, thousands of pets
Rabbits, dogs, cats and fish.
I like all kinds of pets.

Rebecca Austin (8)
Gunthorpe Primary School

The Tree Poem

The powerful tree has been there for years
Standing tired and weary
Swaying like the sea
The hard, brown trunk
Wise, the greatest tree of all
The powerful tree has been wise and working for 50 years
Hearing all the peoples' secrets.

The tired, crooked tree
Standing for years
Swaying like a flag
Like a flag.

Alicia Breen (7)
Gunthorpe Primary School

In Gunthorpe's Area

In Gunthorpe's area, cars were whizzing past,
In Gunthorpe's area, cars were going fast.
In Gunthorpe's area, shops were busy too,
In Gunthorpe's area, I heard a bird going, *'Cuckoo!'*

In Gunthorpe's area, the parks were full of fun,
In Gunthorpe's area, I saw someone going for a run.

Jordan Singleton (8)
Gunthorpe Primary School

The Tree

The tree is fifty years old,
The tree is ancient,
The tree is wise,
The tree is powerful,
The tree is strong and healthy.

Jordan Dorling (9)
Gunthorpe Primary School

The Tree

The tree is fifty years old
The poor tree is nearly dead
It's about to fall to the soft ground.
The wise tree is sad
He knows he's one step away from death
Until the acorn drops
And buries itself in the ground
And a new tree grows.

Ryan Humphreys (8)
Gunthorpe Primary School

Ice Skating

When you ice skate you glide,
It swipes you off your feet,
It's like flying around the room,
You will get the hang of it.
I love to ice skate,
It's fun, fun, fun,
You try it, you will enjoy it,
Like I said, it's a fun thing.

Imogen Lara Breen (8)
Gunthorpe Primary School

The Life Of A Tree

The tree standing as tall as a giraffe,
As old as a grandad,
As hard as a bone,
As friendly as a fish,
As skinny as a person,
Crunchy leaves falling,
Falling as light as a feather.

Kerry Camwell (9)
Gunthorpe Primary School

A Monster In Wicken Fen

They declare there's a monster at Wicken Fen,
He slithers like a hunting snake
Ready to get its prey.

He lives in a burrow and he's *enormous!*
At Wicken Fen, it's creepy at night
But very deserted.

They declare there's a monster at Wicken Fen,
At Wicken Fen he's eaten people,
Fish, cars and houses.

Kieran Brooks (9)
Gunthorpe Primary School

The Ancient Tree

I am still standing here,
Ninety years have gone,
I have so many memories till
I am finally gone.

I am still standing here,
As rough as the sea,
I have got a heavy trunk,
Just like you and the other tree.

Tara Arden (7)
Gunthorpe Primary School

Mad Monster

There was a monster from Leeds,
Who ate a packet of seeds,
In less than an hour,
His nose was a flower,
And his head was a garden of weeds!

Lauren Woods (9)
Gunthorpe Primary School

The Life Of A Tree

Branches like waving arms and legs.
Growing like a little baby, into a grown-up.
Banging on the window, like speaking.
Swaying from side to side.
Walking and dropping leaves like dying.
As old as the Queen.
As young as a newborn baby.
As beautiful as a flower.
As thin as a giraffe's neck.
As friendly as a home pet.

Gabriele Nauyte (9)
Gunthorpe Primary School

The Tree

One tree, just one, tall, thick tree
Swaying proudly in the breeze.
It looks over Gunthorpe Primary School.
Every day, children look up at the tree
And it looks like it waves at them.
The tree stands tall and wise and powerful.
The tree is very neighbourly and kind.
As it gets older, it grows wiser.
It is older by the minute.
It is enchanted.

Bradley Alan Street (8)
Gunthorpe Primary School

The Tree

The tall tree dying on the field,
Fifty years still standing,
The magical tree standing for years,
Now it's come to an end for the beautiful tree,
It smashes to the ground after fifty years.

Aimee Griffin (8)
Gunthorpe Primary School

The Tree

The tree was bendy and wavy
Swishing around in the wind
The tree is really skinny and waving
Like a friendly tree
A lovely tree whistling through the night
A still, stout tree shivering in the fields
You are a tree, little and weak
You are a new tree in the playground
As small as a six-year-old child
You look as if one touch would snap you
As proud as a cat running around
The big field by the tree.

Georgia Kendall (8)
Gunthorpe Primary School

Stubborn Brother

Mathew looked at the moon at night,
How could it be so bright?
'Hey, Bella, do you know about the moon?
But how could you know about it so soon?'

'Yes, I do know about the moon,
It's made of cheese.'

'No, it's made of dust,
It's you I can't trust,
Because I was putting you to the test
And I know that I'm the best.'

'You know it's cheese,
It's just for you to please.'

Keira Nicholl (10)
Old Fletton Primary School

Aliens Are Here!

Aliens have landed!
What am I to do?
They just came down
In the downtown zoo.

I went to tell the zookeeper
About what they'd done,
But when we turned around,
All of the animals had gone!

Then I went to search
To see where they were,
But I got caught up
Wondering what they were.

I finally got to see them
And they looked a bit gooey,
But when I looked again,
The goo looked chewy!

When the aliens went,
They all said bye,
But then I started to wonder
How the spaceship could fly.

Chris Goodrum (10)
Old Fletton Primary School

Space

S uper, sizzling Saturn
P etrified, pitch-black Pluto
A stonishing, amazing asteroids
C olourful, colossal comets
E rupting, everlasting Earth.

Karl Broughton (10) & Ben George (9)
Old Fletton Primary School

Saturn, The Suspicious Planet

S aturn, big, stripy, rotating planet
A stronauts taking photos of this amazing wonder
T winkling stars all around it
U p above we see it so high
R ising up in the night-time sky
N othing left, just Saturn and I.

Shannon Murtagh (9)
Old Fletton Primary School

The Thing On The Fridge

Last night I heard a crash, a bang and a wallop,
So I went to investigate.
I went down the stairs and into the kitchen
And sitting there on our fridge was a . . .
Spotty, dotty, slimy, sloppy,
Three-eyed, sparkly alien
And he said, 'Breep, breep.'

Katie Hibbins (10)
Old Fletton Primary School

Alien On Mars

Small little alien walking on Mars,
Then he sits down watching the stars.
He saw a comet heading for Mars,
So he got in his spaceship
And flew past the stars.

Daniella Hodge (9)
Old Fletton Primary School

Jupiter

J upiter is cold,
U ranus is big,
P luto is small,
I nvisible aliens,
T urning every day,
E arth is spinning,
R ound and round in every way!

Jade Frisby (9)
Old Fletton Primary School

Uranus

U nstoppable Uranus
R apidly going round
A musing other planets
N ever will
U ranus amuses the
S un because the sun's too hot.

Kieran Read (9)
Old Fletton Primary School

Alien And Me

Passing past Neptune, here we go,
Me and spotty-dotty alien,
With Earth down below.
We met back on Jupiter on the 1st of July,
Spotty-dotty and I watched the planets go by.

Bethany Schofield (9)
Old Fletton Primary School

The Visitors

An alien came to my door one day,
With his friends he asked me to play.
He was green and slimy, with one eye on his head,
'I can't come out tonight,' I said, 'I have to go to bed.'
My mum came down and screamed out loud,
'What on earth are you doing hanging out with an
                                        out of this world crowd?'

Konnor Greenhow (10)
Old Fletton Primary School

Mars

M ysterious Mars,
A mazing asteroids,
R ight up high,
S oaring through the night sky.

Sophie Holman (10)
Old Fletton Primary School

Stars, Stars

S tars, stars, stars so bright,
T winkle, twinkle all the night.
A s they light up the sky,
R ight up on high,
S parkling stars watch the world spin and go by.

Eleanor McMullon (10)
Old Fletton Primary School

Fried Alien

An alien walking through space,
Carrying his case,
Chucked out of his home,
Has nowhere to go.
But then he sees a light,
So bright.
Walks towards the shiny light,
Steps on top of the light,
He gave me a fright.
All fried up for my tea,
But all that is left are his smelly shoes.

Olivia Taylor (9)
Old Fletton Primary School

Earth

E verlasting, extraordinary, exciting Earth,
A stronauts, asteroids, atmosphere, astronomers,
R ather rapid razor rocket,
T he twizzling, twisting tracker,
H overing, hastily, heavenly, home.

Lewis Trundell (10)
Old Fletton Primary School

Stars

S tars twinkle in the night sky
T hey help the moon to light up the galaxy
A stronauts gaze at their beauty
R eal diamonds on a black, velvet sky.

Jordan Turner (10)
Old Fletton Primary School

Aliens

A bandoned, abnormal aliens
L arge, luminous UFOs
I cy, interesting Saturn
E arth is dodging asteroids
N eptune is cold and freezing
S pace is scary, but sparkly.

Lauren Thorndyke (9)
Old Fletton Primary School

Space Race

Space is a place where aliens race,
Past red planet Mars in their alien cars.
Skidding on Saturn's rings, flapping their wings,
Passing by Pluto to the finishing post.
There's no better place than great outer space.

Aimee Rotundi (10)
Old Fletton Primary School

With Fear As I Walk In Space

S hivering with fear as I walk in space
P luto and planets all around me
A steroids flying towards Earth
C ircling, sparkling stars light up the sky
E mpty black holes trying to suck me in.

Albert Johnson (9)
Old Fletton Primary School

Uranus

U ntouchable, unique Uranus
R ings of light rapidly rotating
A liens invading Earth
N ewly nibbled Neptune
U ltimate, unstoppable sun
S tripy, stringy sunrays.

Adam Canham (10)
Old Fletton Primary School

Space

S wirling, twirling Saturn
P retty, patterned Pluto
A dventurous, abandoned Mars
C ircling, colossal comet
E verlasting, extraordinary Earth.

Craig Sayer (9)
Old Fletton Primary School

Space

S weaty, swirling sun,
P itch-black, painstaking Pluto,
A mazing, adventurous asteroid,
C reepy, creaky comets,
E ventually, everlasting Earth.

Safia Djaballah (9)
Old Fletton Primary School

The Sun

The sun is like a ball of fire,
The sun is scorching,
The sun hovers over the Earth.
It looks like it has got a red face,
If you went near it, it would burn you.
The sun hasn't got any friends,
It is always lonely.
It is born in the summer
And dies in the winter.

Shannon Papworth
Parnwell Primary School

Forest

I am as tall as giants,
My legs are big and cold,
So my arms tangle and twist,
I am as still as bricks,
All my days have been silent and still,
I am lonely and abandoned,
Forever.

Benjamin Quigley (10)
Parnwell Primary School

The Stars

The stars are shining diamonds in the sky,
Disappearing in the morning
And coming out at night with the moon.

The sun glides through the day
And the moon walks with the stars at night.

Luke Sharpe
Parnwell Primary School

The Forest

I am a soulless mind of a graveyard,
Motionless, like an empty heart,
My dead colours reflect my dark feelings,
Abandoned like a lost child.
I am as petrifying as a dementor,
Darkest of all omens.
The dark dusk dawns upon me,
Beyond the darkness there lies . . .
Me.

Hayley Lawrence (11)
Parnwell Primary School

The Sun

He is hot and blinding,
He is the hot sphere,
He is as bright as a spotlight,
He heats up the land,
He is the light of the night,
He is a scorching ball of fire,
He is a blistering hot desert.

Ashley Clarke (11)
Parnwell Primary School

The Sun

I am a big, golden disc of fire,
I am a hot dish of spicy vindaloo,
I drink flames and spit out the heat,
I travel around the world burning a bright light.

Jacquelyn Carlton (11)
Parnwell Primary School

The Wind

The wind is like a cheetah,
Racing through villages and rivers.
The wind's hands slap trees and houses
To cause calamity.
The wind whooshes and howls at passers by.
The wind is a demon,
Running around cackling,
Stirring up trouble.
The wind blusters here and there,
Until everything's gone.
Dead!

Fiona King (11)
Parnwell Primary School

The Wind

I am the wind,
I gush gracefully,
I howl like a dog
I chatter constantly,
I flow quickly,
I dance with my feet,
I play with the leaves,
I am the wind.

Claire Ravenhill (11)
Parnwell Primary School

Forest

The forest is dark and frightening.
It is silent, abandoned.
The gigantic trees block out the sunlight.
The leather leaves float off the trees.
Eyes like the moon's glow.
He is gloomy, but greedy for air.

Alex Wright (10)
Parnwell Primary School

The Sea

The mother of all lakes
Her arms guide the swimmers to safety
Carrying sticks along with the tide
Beach balls stranded in her grip
Plastic bags floating in her ocean.
Her eyes watch us as we swim
The warmth of the sea attracts children from far and wide.
She is glum and lonely but we are her friends
Her waves are not rough, but they are calm
She may be wavy now and then.
She is a blaze of flashing blue
She sits and waits for the time to move, leaving behind slushy mud.
She is wet and sometimes cold, but we still have fun.
She loves the sound of the happy seagulls
She makes the crashing on the rocks
Boats come and go, we all love the sea.
The sea is happy, although she is lonely
She is blue but never only one shade of blue.
The sea is full of pollution
All of your old, smelly nappies and plastic bottles.
I run away from small children providing them with a safe place
to swim.

Lying flat with no bumps or bruises
I am bumpy only when I am grumpy
I am only grumpy when I am misled.

Amy Gilbert (11)
Parnwell Primary School

The Misty Moon

She stalks through the dark,
Gloomy and shouting out to the stars like a predator
And waking us with her roar,
Shaking the Earth of the day,
She is a glow of fear.

David Toon (11)
Parnwell Primary School

Wrath

The sun is scorching hot,
It's a non-stop flame,
That none can tame.
The sun can burn the lot,
The sun is scared of the night,
The moon burns out the sun's light.

Holly Gallacher (11)
Parnwell Primary School

Sonic

S peeding
O ver the ground
N othing to stop him
I ncredible
C hasing bad guys.

Kierran Porter
Parnwell Primary School

Birds

B eautiful birds
I n the trees
R eady for singing
D rinking water
S wooping.

Alfie Smith
Parnwell Primary School

Flower Haiku Poem

Pretty, bright roses
Wind blowing them to each side
On a bright, hot day.

Bernadette Wysockyj
Parnwell Primary School

Joseph

J oseph had a coat of many colours
O verjoyed was Joseph when he got his new coat
S trange dreams Joseph dreamt
E leven brothers hated Joseph
P ushed into prison, Joseph fell
H ungry people came to Joseph in Egypt.

Dorinda Vosloo (8)
Parnwell Primary School

Snail

S nails are the best
N ever stop going
A slow mover
I ts home is on its back
L eaving a silver trail.

Jacqueline Jones (7)
Parnwell Primary School

Wind

The wind crashes into the trees,
The wind is as angry as thunder,
The wind is as strong as a wrestler,
The wind is as fast as lightning,
It dies when summer comes.

Kayleigh Daulton (10)
Parnwell Primary School

Dolphin Haiku

Blue, friendly dolphins,
Crashing through the cold water,
When the sunset comes.

Rachael Smith (10)
Parnwell Primary School

Wind

The wind blows,
As the trees whisper
And the seas shiver.

The wind growls angrily
As it moves through the dark woods,
Huffing as it goes.

The wind has eyes like a devil,
Breath like snow,
A growl like a lion,
With big, sharp, icicle lips
And deep, dark death at his back.

The wind disappears
As the spring sun pushes its way out
And dries all the rain and snow out.

Kirstie Denton
Parnwell Primary School

Space

S tars shining
P lenty of planets
A blazing sun
C raters on the moon
E veryone stares.

Connor Jones (8)
Parnwell Primary School

Tiger

T onight I go sneaking through the leaves
I n the dark, dark breeze
G o back to my cave
E very tiger is fierce
R oar! We shout every night.

Rebecca Smith (8)
Parnwell Primary School

My Mum

She is a glistening chandelier that never goes out,
She's a soft kitten that's good for a laugh,
She is a golden palace and a shining star,
She's the sound of nature that you never forget,
She's the moonlight that glows,
She is the sherry that's pink, bright and clear.

Rebecca Blackledge (10)
Parnwell Primary School

My Friend

She's a strong, shiny table,
She's a bright bumblebee,
A strong, loud whirlwind,
She's as wild as a waterfall,
She's a fiery sunset, red and orange,
She's a strong cup of coffee.

Amy Wright (10)
Parnwell Primary School

Tiger Haiku

A dark, scary tiger,
When they jump on top of you,
On a dark, cold day.

Luke Oorloff & Dalton Leedell (9)
Parnwell Primary School

Sea Haiku

A nice, calm, deep sea,
Gentle, calm, relaxing sea,
On a hot summer's day.

Lauren Clark (9)
Parnwell Primary School

This Is Just To Say - A Reply

(Based on 'This Is Just To Say' by William Carlos Williams)

This is just to say
I am forgiving,
You ate the plums
That were in the icebox

And I was saving them
For my breakfast

Don't worry,
I have more
That are
So delicious,
So sweet
And so cold.

Jan Zamirski (10)
Perse Preparatory School

Beyond The Door

(Based on 'The Door' by Miroslav Holob)

Go and open the door
Maybe outside there's
An eagle or a dragon,
A city,
Or a pile of gold glistening.

Go and open the door,
Maybe there's an archer,
Maybe there's a deadly snake,
Or a pit,
Or a knight battling.
If you see a dragon,
It will eat you alive.

Dominic Barrett (8)
Perse Preparatory School

This Is Just To Say - A Reply

(Based on 'This Is Just To Say' by William Carlos Williams)

William Carlos Williams
I am sorry to say
These plums are 100 days
Old from today.

They are very much off
And will make you cough
And the icebox has got
A nest of spiders.

William Carlos Williams
Thank you for eating them
I was wondering what to do with them
Probably going to throw them away.

They cost 20p
Which is a lot for me
I'm certainly glad I didn't waste them
Thank you William Carlos Williams, thank you.

Matthew Evans (9)
Perse Preparatory School

This Is Just To Say - A Reply

(Based on 'This Is Just To Say' by William Carlos Williams)

This is just to say
The plums you ate from the icebox
Were for brother
As a well done gift from us.

Mama was angry
But I know you were
Out all night
You deserved them.

George Davies (9)
Perse Preparatory School

This Is Just To Say - Reply

(Based on 'This Is Just To Say' by William Carlos Williams)

Me . . .   It's OK you ate the plums
             Because you are my mate

Him . . .   Just to confess
             These plums are the best
             These plums are ripe
             Could you get some by night?

Me . . .   I can get some
             Because they're not far away
             You deserve these plums
             You sit at night
             With your eyes open wide
             Reading and reading
             And reading.

Priyan Davda (9)
Perse Preparatory School

This Is Just To Say - A Reply

(Based on 'This Is Just To Say' by William Carlos Williams)

This is just to say
It's alright you
Ate the plums.

They were really for you
I didn't like them
I saved them for you.

I forgive you
I think they were horrible
Because I don't like plums!

Harry Claydon (9)
Perse Preparatory School

This Is Just To Say, You're Welcome

(Based on 'This Is Just To Say' by William Carlos Williams)

Dear William Carlos Williams
Don't worry
About plums
In the icebox

Help yourself to the
Garden plums
That sway
So freely on the tree

Little plums
In a kitchen
Don't worry
Me.

By the stranger who lives in the house.

Fergus Waugh (9)
Perse Preparatory School

This Is Just To Say - A Reply

(Based on 'This Is Just To Say' by William Carlos Williams)

This is just to say
It's okay
There's some more outside

So sweet
So cold
So delicious

And I do not mind
They are for you
Just you.

Joshua Walker (9)
Perse Preparatory School

This Is Just To Say - A Reply

(Based on 'This Is Just To Say' by William Carlos Williams)

This is just a reply
To say
The plums
Were for
You.

I do not
Like those
Plums.

I was saving
Them for you
After your hard day's
Work.

I know you
Like plums
As I do not.

Toby Phillips (10)
Perse Preparatory School

This Is Just To Say - A Reply

(Based on 'This Is Just To Say' by William Carlos Williams)

I am glad
You ate the plums
Because they were from
The poisoned plum tree.

They were so sweet and delicious
Because I put some sugar on them
And a magic spell.

From Aunt Betty.

William Thwaites (10)
Perse Preparatory School

This Is A Letter To Say It's OK

(Based on 'This Is Just To Say' by William Carlos Williams)

That is OK
I didn't really
Want them
Anyway

There are lots
More on the
Tree outside

You deserve them
You have been working
So hard
For me

Don't worry
You must have been
Starving.

Jonathan Heybrock (9)
Perse Preparatory School

This Is Just To Say - A Reply

(Based on 'This Is Just To Say' by William Carlos Williams)

This is just to say . . .
It's okay about the plums,
I can always buy more.

You deserve them more than I do,
You have probably been awake all night,
So I think you should have had them.

Ollie McLellan (10)
Perse Preparatory School

This Is Just To Say - A Reply

(Based on 'This Is Just To Say' by William Carlos Williams)

This is just to say
I don't mind if you've
Eaten the plums,
They were rotten anyway.

We were waiting
For you to eat the plums
I prefer strawberries
What about you?

I find it fascinating
How every night
You come into the kitchen
And yet I still play
That trick on you.

Tom O'Keefe (10)
Perse Preparatory School

This Is Just To Say

(Based on 'This Is Just To Say' by William Carlos Williams)

I am sorry to say
That I was saving them for today
They looked so juicy
But alas, now they are gone

We had a guest coming
An important one at that
Those juicy, ripe plums
Were going to be his
As a going away present
It doesn't sound like much
But it's all we had left.

Oliver Linehan (9)
Perse Preparatory School

This Is Just To Say - A Reply

(Based on 'This Is Just To Say' by William Carlos Williams)

This is just to say
You have eaten
My plums
That were in
My icebox.

I'm angry
Because I was going
To eat my plums
For breakfast.

No forgiving
Not delicious
Not sweet
And not cold.

Huw Oliver (10)
Perse Preparatory School

This Is Just To Say - A Reply

(Based on 'This Is Just To Say' by William Carlos Williams)

This is just to say,
That I forgive you, Father
And I understand that you were tired
And I understand that you were hungry,
So you could not resist
Eating those plums
In the icebox.

This is just to say,
That I forgive you, Father.

Alan Kanapin (9)
Perse Preparatory School

This Is Just To Say - A Reply

(Based on 'This Is Just To Say' by William Carlos Williams)

This is just to say,
It is OK.
They were for you.
Did you like
The plums
In the icebox?

I was going to
Eat them for
Breakfast,
If you
Had not taken them,
Like I hoped.

I hope they were
Delicious,
Sweet and
Cold.

Alec Jenkins (10)
Perse Preparatory School

This Is Just To Say - A Reply

(Based on 'This Is Just To Say' by William Carlos Williams)

I am sorry to say
Those plums were
For me and my
Brother and they
Were very
Special.

Now I cannot share
Those ripe, lovely
Plums with my brother,
My favourite brother.

Joe Harper (10)
Perse Preparatory School

Beyond The Door

(Based on 'The Door' by Miroslav Holub)

Go and open the door,
Maybe outside there's
A flag or a king
Swords clashing
Or a breeze in the wind.

Go and open the door,
Maybe there's a horse
Maybe with a stable close by
Or a rider riding fast
Or a blacksmith shoeing a horse.

Go and open the door,
If you win you will be declared champion!
It will hurt if you lose!

Ben Murray (7)
Perse Preparatory School

This Is Just To Say - A Reply

(Based on 'This Is Just To Say' by William Carlos Williams)

That I salute you for your courage, for
Staying up all night.

I admire you, take anything you want
It is all yours.

You are a model, that no patient of yours will forget
I forgive you, good man.

Even if the plums were for the Queen
I would give them to you.

You should be proud of yourself.

Alex Fanourakis (10)
Perse Preparatory School

A Door

(Based on 'The Door' by Miroslav Holub)

Go and open the door.
Maybe outside there's
A flock of birds,
Or a volcano,
A mountain,
Or a field.
Go and open the door.
Maybe a planet,
Maybe a snowy place,
Or a baby penguin,
Or a cat purring.
Go and open the door.
If it was a fine day,
You would have a good view.

James Cockain (8)
Perse Preparatory School

Playground

P laying in the playground is really fun
L ately, I lost my blazer in the playground
A t morning break and lunchtime I play football
Y esterday we lost the game
G *oal!* Someone had scored
R ipped knee in someone's trousers because he fell over
O ut in the football area, crazy footballers argue
U nder the trees we hide
N aughty boys jump out of the window
D rat! I missed the goal!

Bartu Atamert (7)
Perse Preparatory School

Beyond The Door
(Based on 'The Door' by Miroslav Holub)

Go and open the door.
Maybe outside there's
A blue whale,
A great white shark,
Or maybe an octopus.

Go and open the door.
Maybe I'll ride a dolphin,
Maybe feed a blue whale
Or watch a pufferfish,
Or maybe escape a poisonous octopus.

Go and open the door.
If you see a dolphin,
It will let you swim with it.

Ethan Abraham (8)
Perse Preparatory School

Playground

P eople shouting, 'Get that now!'
L unchtime comes, yum, yum, yum!
A lot of people are looking for their coats.
'Y ou,' says the teacher, 'minus point.'
G oals, goals! Pass the ball!
R unning races, pant, pant, pant!
O ver by the drinking fountain
U gly boys drink, drink, drink.
N othing will stop us having fun . . . until the
D oors close at start of school.

Tom Harwood (8)
Perse Preparatory School

Beyond The Door

(Based on 'The Door' by Miroslav Holub)

Go and open the door.
Maybe outside there's
A chocolate city,
Or a giant toffee,
A thousand lollipops,
Or lots of sherbet dips.

Go and open the door.
Maybe there are giant ice cream villages,
Maybe the ice cream van will be there,
Or a milkshake well,
Or burning marshmallows.

Go and open the door.
If it rains,
It will be every sweet you could ever eat!

Nihal Chadha (8)
Perse Preparatory School

Playground

P laying cricket on a sunny day
L aughing, shouting, having fun
A ll over the tarmac children run
Y ellow tennis balls flying through the air
G oal posts are stripy blazers
R uns are scored in ones, fours and sixes
'O ut!' shouts the umpire. 'You're out!'
U pset player walks away sadly
N aughty boys kick the ball away
D ecision is made - they can't play.

Chris Pepper (8)
Perse Preparatory School

Beyond The Door

(Based on 'The Door' by Miroslav Holub)

Go and open the door.
Maybe outside there's
A hot beach with people sunbathing
Or eating picnics and ice creams.
Go and open the door.
Maybe there's some people surfing,
Maybe there are some people swimming,
Or children making sandcastles,
Or yachts on the sea.
Go and open the door.
If you bring a towel,
It will be lovely to go for a swim.

Leo Bridger (8)
Perse Preparatory School

Playground

P eople running up and down in the playground
L ots of tennis balls flying through the air
A dozen people looking for their blazers
Y elling boys - 'Pass that ball to me!'
G oals being scored, maybe even a hat trick
R unning round in circles avoiding who is 'it'
O ut of the bush - 'I've been found'
'U m . . . I didn't do it'
N aughty boys climbing in through the window
D oors close, everything is quiet.

Alex Gilbertson (8)
Perse Preparatory School

Beyond The Door

(Based on 'The Door' by Miroslav Holub)

Go and open the door.
Maybe outside there's
A fish eating,
Or seaweed swaying,
A crab moving,
Or a starfish laying.

Go and open the door.
Maybe there's a shark,
Maybe a lobster sleeping,
Or a water spider making his web,
Or a puff fish puffing up.

Go and open the door.
If there's a wave,
It will kill the seaweed.

Alexander Wilfert (8)
Perse Preparatory School

Playground

P assing, the most important thing
L azy people sucking lollipops
A brilliant shot, just goin' wide
Y awning, tired 3'S waiting for the bell
G oals will not stop a-coming
R iding cycles coming through the playground
O f course boys will score goals
U s boys are running races
N o one can stop us having fun
D readful sixers kicking balls away.

Akbar Akhter (8)
Perse Preparatory School

The Door

(Based on 'The Door' by Miroslav Holub)

Go and open the door.
Maybe outside there's
A classroom,
A sports field,
Or a French room,
Or computers.

Go and open the door.
Maybe people are working,
Maybe people are playing,
Or getting changed,
Or eating biscuits.

Go and open the door.
If it is Thursday,
It will be double games.

Ben Winfield (7)
Perse Preparatory School

Playground

P erse Prep boys having fun,
L aughing and sitting in the hot sun.
A ll alone isn't nice to be,
Y ou feel sad when you've no friends.
G ames to play, like having a race,
R unning away to hide my face.
O pen your milk and have a drink,
U pset I feel when people are mean.
'N ot fair!' someone cries,
D oor closes - it's the end of break.

David Y C Lau (7)
Perse Preparatory School

Beyond The Door

(Based on 'The Door' by Miroslav Holub)

Go and open the door.
Maybe outside there's
A ghost spooking you out,
A body,
Or a ghost haunting you,
Or a witch screaming.

Go and open the door.
Maybe bats will fly past you,
Maybe you will see Frankenstein,
Or a headless ghost,
Or Einstein working.

Go and open the door.
If it is scary,
It will freak you out!

Dominic Strandmann (8)
Perse Preparatory School

Playground

P eople playfighting with each other
L azy children sitting around
A good football player scoring lots of goals
Y awning fivers must be very tired
'G round, ground, *please* don't hurt me!'
R unning races in the playground
O utstanding cricket players score lots of runs
U nder the drain the ball goes rolling
N aughty children smack their friends
D oomed people do hand balls!

Conor Sullivan (7)
Perse Preparatory School

Beyond The Door
(Based on 'The Door' by Miroslav Holub)

Go and open the door.
Maybe outside there's
A battlefield,
Or a barracks,
A castle,
Or a fort.

Go and open the door.
Maybe knights are charging,
Maybe swords are clashing,
Or arrows are shooting,
Or javelins flying.

Go and open the door.
If an army wins,
It will be in peace.

Henry Gregory (8)
Perse Preparatory School

Playground

P assing the ball in football matches
L aughing and dancing makes the game
A lways running wins the fame
Y ack, yack, yack! As people dance into line
G oals for everyone who likes football
R oaring and hitting the ball towards the target
'O h no! My ball's gone over!' and you start to cry
U s boys go around playing chasing games
N othing will stop us from having fun
D oors slam, then quiet when it's the end of break.

Alex Mitchell (7)
Perse Preparatory School

Beyond The Door

(Based on 'The Door' by Miroslav Holub)

Go and open the door.
Maybe outside there's
A scorpion stinging people,
Or a ghost,
A spider eating its prey,
Or a snake strangling loads of things.

Go and open the door.
Maybe there's a basilisk,
Maybe there's a vampire sucking blood,
Or a man with his brain out of his head,
Or one million bees stinging someone.

Go and open the door.
If you go in,
It will freak you out!

Hugh O'Keefe (8)
Perse Preparatory School

Playground

P layground
L ovely places!
A ctivities all round the school
Y our tennis ball is used for football
G usty weather round you
R ambling boys, playing football
O f course they will score a goal!
U s boys are running races
N aughty boys kick and punch
D own the playground we roam!

Hugh Goddard (7)
Perse Preparatory School

Beyond The Door

(Based on 'The Door' by Miroslav Holub)

Go and open the door.
Maybe outside there's
A city with loud traffic,
Crowded streets,
Or long queues for ice cream.

Go and open the door.
Maybe there is a theatre,
Maybe traffic lights flashing,
Or a sweet shop with candy,
Or a football stadium.

Go and open the door.
If you enter the town,
It will be very crowded.

Owen Good (8)
Perse Preparatory School

Playground

P eople passing and scoring goals
L azy boys sitting on the bench
A nd lots of fourers squabbling over free kicks
Y elling boys scream and shout
G roaning sixers wait for their lunch
R unning, mad people in a frenzy
O ver the wall flies a shoe!
U nder the tree we go
N oisy boys play and shout
D oors shut and play ends.

Mycroft Majumdar (8)
Perse Preparatory School

Beyond The Door

(Based on 'The Door' by Miroslav Holub)

Go and open the door.
Maybe outside there's
A cricket bat,
Or a football,
A basketball match,
Or a cricket match.

Go and open the door.
Maybe you get out,
Maybe you score a goal,
Or you get a century,
Or you save a goal.

If I get 401,
It will mean I am a cricket world record holder!

Mohammed Zia (8)
Perse Preparatory School

Playground

P eople shouting loudly
L ucky boys scoring their goals
A ngry teachers helping the injured
Y ou're lining up for a biscuit at break
'G reat goal! Great goal!' people shout
R unning round the playground
O bjects aren't in our way
U sing tennis balls for a game
N aughty boys getting minus points
D aring, naughty boys being seen by teachers.

Thomas Poskitt (8)
Perse Preparatory School

Beyond The Door

(Based on 'The Door' by Miroslav Holub)

Go and open the door.
Maybe outside there's
A ghost or zombie,
A head or an ugly witch.

Go and open the door.
Maybe a mummy's sleeping,
Maybe a monster's thinking,
Or there's a moving picture,
Or repulsive slime.

Go and open the door.
If you see the ghost train,
It will give you a ride!

Edward Chadwick (8)
Perse Preparatory School

Playground

P eople playing with older brothers
L aughing boys chasing each other
A lost pencil waits to be found
Y elling children in the playground
G rumbling when not allowed to play
R unning very fast all through the day
O nto the roof goes the tennis ball
U nder a tree people play, hoping it won't fall
N aughty children get a telling off
D inner break comes, then the boys go scoff!

Christopher Stone (8)
Perse Preparatory School

Books

I love to curl up with a book,
Pongwiffy, Potter or Captain Hook.
I wish I could have books galore,
Reading for hours and hours and more.
Under my covers, flashlight in hand,
Ratty and Mole and Robin Hood's band.
I cannot finish when Mum says, 'Stop!'
Alex Rider or Hop on Pop.
There's always one more chapter to be read,
Lounging in an armchair or lying in bed.
I open up the cover and what do I see?
A whole wondrous world waiting for me.

Jonathan Marrow (8)
Perse Preparatory School

Playground

P laying like mad are the children
L azy they're not in the playground
A ll at once the bell goes *ring* and the next lesson is PE
'Y ou!' the teacher says. 'Behave!'
'G oal!' says Chris. 'We win!'
R unning races in the grounds
'O h, that stupid boy stole my ball!'
U pset children hide under benches
N aughty children jump through windows
D ozy children rest on benches in the sun.

Remin Harji (7)
Perse Preparatory School

The Tree

The tree is a dancer,
Swaying in the breeze,
It will dance forever,
Full of ease.

The tree's an explorer,
Reaching for the sky,
Birds on his shoulders,
As they pass by.

The tree's a king,
So noble and strong,
When the wind blows hard,
He can't live so long.

Erica Davletov (10)
Queen Edith Community Primary School

The River

The river's a traitor,
Never the same,
It's almost as if,
He's playing a game.

The river's a playground,
With a gentle tide,
It's so much fun,
Just like a ride.

The river's a horse,
Always running,
But be careful,
He's ever so cunning.

Alice Gooch (10)
Queen Edith Community Primary School

The Tree

The tree's an innkeeper,
Happy to give
Creatures and insects
A place to live.

The tree's a teacher,
Wise and old,
Telling the tales
Which have never been told.

The tree's almighty,
He does what he pleases,
He can bend and twist,
And grab with ease.

The tree's a trader,
He gives and he takes,
He shows us his wonder,
The beauty he makes.

Cordelia Chui (9)
Queen Edith Community Primary School

The Tree

The tree's a home to all the birds and creatures
With plants and blossoms
To make great features.

The tree's an airport
For all the birds to land,
But then they'll take off later
And fly to another land.

The tree's a soldier
Standing very still,
But if you're very silly,
It's big enough to kill.

Rishi Verma (9)
Queen Edith Community Primary School

I Am . . .

I am an animal that has a long tail,
Squeak, squeak,
I am a mouse!

I am an animal that has fins,
Bubble, bubble,
I am a fish!

I am an animal that likes to hop,
Hop, hop,
I am a rabbit!

I am an animal flying in the air,
Tweet, tweet,
I am a bird!

I am an animal that chases cats,
Woof, woof,
I am a dog!

I am a human being,
On Earth,
I am Thomas!

Thomas Rice (7)
Walton Junior School

The Rain Story

Mizzle drizzle
Floating from the sky
Pitter-patter sprinkle
Falling from the sky
Drip drop splash
Pouring from the sky
Monsoon of cats and dogs
Pelting from the sky
Outside it's waterlogged
Quiet relaxing rivers
Flowing on the ground.

Sam-Luca Rolph (7)
Walton Junior School

Tsunami

As we woke up on Boxing Day
The news was not so good.
A country that was far away
Had suffered a terrible flood.

A gigantic wave from far out at sea
Had started on its way
It hit the coast with such mighty force
Which caused a catastrophe.

The adults and children ran for their lives
Not knowing where to go
Their houses and homes were washed away
As the water began to flow.

Hundreds and thousands were killed that day
So many will not be found
The water took them all out to sea
The fear is they all have drowned.

So now the work begins to repair the damage done
Let us all give our fair share
And pray that God will give back the beauty
To these islands in the sun.

Olivia Margaret Hogan (8)
Walton Junior School

Sun

Sun is bright
Sun is delight
To see it smile
All the while
Go and have fun
So just play in the sun
Don't spend time to look
Don't spend time to cook
Go and have fun
So just play in the sun.

Joshua Saville (7)
Walton Junior School

The Disaster

The smell of smoke and fire,
A shouting and screaming choir,
The sound of crackling,
Fire tackling.

Samuel Peeps ran to the king,
As the fire bells go ding-a-ling-ling.
It was dark and black outside,
People ran away on the tide.

In the end there were no flowers,
No houses,
No towers.

Now it is Friday and the fire has ended,
The houses and the towers in time are mended.

Megan Somers (8)
Walton Junior School

Rain Poem

Rain on the window, rain on the ground,
Rain over there and rain all around.
Rain is coming, got to dash,
Halfway there . . . *splash!*

I'm in bed as still as a log,
It's not raining yet, it's just fog.
I hope it tip-taps on the windowpane,
Come on, come on, come out rain.

I am a lonely raindrop,
I need to find some friends,
When I join the others,
My friendship will never end.

Joshua Hales (7)
Walton Junior School

Lightning

I was in my bed that night
When the lightning flashed and flickered fast at me
Through a gap in my curtains.

I screamed with horror and fear.
I hid under the quilt trembling,
Hoping that it would stop.
I fell asleep to bangs, crashes and flashes.

Next day I woke up after the storm had gone.
It was a sunny morning and all was calm.
I had my breakfast and trotted off to school
As if nothing had happened at all.

Glen Thompson (7)
Walton Junior School

I'm Dreaming Of A Faraway Place

I'm dreaming of a place
It's far away,
Guess, go on guess,
Bet you don't know.
Am I princess,
Or a queen?
Yeah, you got it,
I'm a princess,
In a faraway castle.

Georgia Armfield (8)
Walton Junior School

My Puppy, Bernie

When Bernie plays with his bone, he chew-chews.
When Bernie is excited, his tail goes wag-waggle.
When Bernie wants a snooze, I give him hug-huggles.

Noah Bell (8)
Walton Junior School

My Cat

My cat is a very fat chap,
We rub his tummy
And he thinks it's funny.
He is black and white
And sleeps all day and night.
He is very lazy
And a little crazy.
He watches telly,
Whilst licking his belly.
He is my best friend,
Even though he drives me round the bend.

Asha Green (7)
Walton Junior School

I'm Someone

I'm someone who keeps you safe,
I give you food and water.

I'm someone who won't let you go,
I'm someone who's part of your life.

I'm someone who helps you with your problems,
I'm someone who protects you.

It's your mum and dad.

Amy Allen (8)
Walton Junior School

What Am I?

Scrap paper torn into bits
Fluffy blankets of white
I am cold, but fun
And you don't get much of me.

I am snow.

Charlotte Griffin (8)
Walton Junior School

Lucky

My pet Lucky
Gets very, very mucky.
He's white and black,
Very fat,
With a flat nose
And his little white toes.
He hops around
All over the ground.

My pet Lucky
Is nibbly
And nosey,
Sometimes very, very cosy.
He has a habit
Of chewing the wire
Near the fire!

What's my pet?

Sabrina Giordano (7)
Walton Junior School

What Am I?

I'm tiny and cute
Sweet and cuddly
Soft ginger fur
Twitchy whiskers

My claws are sharp
My teeth are too
The seeds and nibble sticks
I like to chew.

I play at night
Sleep all day
What am I?
Now you can say . . .
Hamster.

Holly Kaminski (7)
Walton Junior School

The Long Holiday Goodbye

I'm going on holiday
I am not joking
I am really going
I have my bags packed
I am going out the door
I have just shut the door
Hold on, I will just do it again to make sure
I'm walking down the street
I am cold
I am scared
It is dark
I want to go home
I run back to my house
I get home and say to myself
I would rather be at home than in the cold.

Tanisha Speechley (7)
Walton Junior School

A Dragon Called Ted

One day I met a dragon,
His name was Ted,
He could not breathe fire,
But I did not care
Because he was such a good friend.
He showed me a secret island,
Guess what was hanging on the trees,
Cookies and ice cream.
He showed me a secret passageway,
Filled with cookie warriors
With their ice cream swords.
What an adventure I had,
I hope there were no veggie warriors.

Joseph Smith (7)
Walton Junior School

Lost On Earth

I am a dark green, wrinkly-skinned blob,
A disgrace to this place they call Earth.

My eyes are yellow and big like flying saucers,
My mouth is rather small.

People here are strange, they all look the same,
They have two legs and arms and only one head.

Not like back at home where my friend Ted
Has three tiny red heads that swivel around and touch the ground.

I look up at the sky and a tear comes to my eye,
I wish I was home.

Can you guess what I am and where I'm from?

Eleanor Jones (7)
Walton Junior School

What Am I?

I am a penguin, as cold as can be
I like to catch fish to eat for my tea.

I like to slide down the hill on my tummy
My friends all laugh and say that I'm funny.

We huddle together to keep ourselves warm
And go to sleep until the dawn.

Daisy Bews (7)
Walton Junior School

Who Am I?

I am as bright as the sun,
As quick as the speed of sound.
I am as strong as a weightlifter,
A shock to the Earth
And you'd better watch out.

Adam Rooney (8)
Walton Junior School

If I Were A . . .

If I were a dolphin,
I'd swim all day long,
Weaving through the seaweed,
Squeaking a happy song.

If I were a hamster,
I'd sleep the day away,
Waking up at night,
To very merrily play.

If I were a seagull,
I'd fly around the sky,
Only stopping to catch a fish
And maybe the odd steak pie!

If I were a rabbit,
I'd hop about all day,
Stopping to eat carrots,
To give me energy to play.

If I were a bumblebee,
I'd spend my day in flowers,
Buzzing here, buzzing there
And playing for hours.

If I were a horse,
I'd be a chestnut mare,
Galloping round the field,
While the people stare.

If I were an animal,
The animal I'd be,
Is *me!*

Chloe Griffin (8)
Walton Junior School

Winter

Winter morning,
Winter night,
Winter frost,
Winter fright.
Winter comes
And leaves some snow,
Then you'll go and play in it,
I know!

Ashlie Coward (8)
Walton Junior School

The Magic Box

(Based on 'Magic Box' by Kit Wright)

I will put in my box . . .
All the magical memories of my nine long years
A world called Gobbledegook that is pale blue all over
A baby dragon's first puff of fire.

I will put in my box . . .
A clever robot that is good at maths
The creak of a door in the midday sun
A fifty-third week with bouncy blue grass.

I will put in my box . . .
The names of every one of my friends
The last words of a dying soldier
One hundred everlasting dreams.

My box is fashioned from the colours of a rainbow
With shiny swirls on the lid
The hinges are made from the strings of a guitar.

I will ski in my box
On the grass in Bombay
Then fly across the world and land in my bed.

Bethany Flack (9)
Wilburton VPC School

The Magic Box

(Based on 'Magic Box' by Kit Wright)

I will put in my box . . .
The bounce of an African kangaroo
A big bite of chocolate CadburyLand
A flying saucer from outer space.

I will put in my box . . .
A trail leading to the end of the world
A huge bite of the biggest candy bar on Earth
And a wizard that does all that I will command.

I will put in my box . . .
A trip around the world in nine days
A three-storey house made out of gold
And a dog only three inches tall.

I will put in my box . . .
A tremendous tree that will talk to me
A piece of cardboard made out of metal
And a pen that will last nine million years.

My box is fashioned from scales of a fish
And dust from the moon and voices in the corners.
Its hinges are made from the bones of an elephant.
The lock is made from unbreakable plastic.

I shall sleep in my box
In the most bounciest bed ever made.
Then I shall wake up in another world
Riding a unicorn.

Hayden Coe (10)
Wilburton VPC School

The Magic Box

(Based on 'Magic Box' by Kit Wright)

I will put in my box . . .
The 36th of May
And the end of a day.
A unicorn riding in an ocean.

I will put in my box . . .
A furry guitar
And a black star,
A flying cat.

I will put in my box . . .
A favourite pop star
And a horse playing the drums.
A monster kind and wide.

My box is styled
From fire, gold and sparkles
And has sounds of angels in the corners.

I will go on an adventure
With a fire breathing snowman,
To the edge of Heaven.

Katie Easton (9)
Wilburton VPC School

The Magic Box

(Based on 'Magic Box' by Kit Wright)

I will put in the box . . .
A dragon's magical breath
A bright star from a dimming sky.

I will put in the box . . .
A baby horse's first neigh
A roar of a dying lion.

I will put in the box . . .
A sound of a sleeping dog
A sprinkle of red grass.

I will put in the box . . .
 A bright white unicorn
A bright silver horseshoe.

My box is covered with diamonds
The corners are covered with horseshoes.

I will ride in my box
On a horse from Australia
To the end of time.

Georgia-May Baylis (10)
Wilburton VPC School

The Magic Box

(Based on 'Magic Box' by Kit Wright)

I will put in the box . . .
The shiny stars in the silver sky,
A newborn butterfly caught by my eye
And a leaping frog jumping about.

I will put in the box . . .
The glory of the summer,
Spreading its wings
And a unicorn riding around.

I will put in the box . . .
Three sparkling wishes,
A fifth season of snow
And the big, bright moon.

I will put in the box . . .
Three beautiful flowers,
A bright yellow beach
And a golden fish.

My box is fashioned
From sequins, diamonds and rubies
With hearts on the lid
And stars in the corners.

I shall surf in my box
The great high mountains
Across the sea
And the cotton clouds.

Coral Gilbert (10)
Wilburton VPC School

The Magic Box

(Based on 'Magic Box' by Kit Wright)

I will put in the box . . .
A giant genie that can make anything true.
A mysterious creature.
A friendly alien who can do absolutely anything.

I will put in the box . . .
A dragon with a very short tail.
A big boat rowing on the long, lonely land.
A snowboard on a half pipe.

I will put in the box . . .
A watery spark.
A twenty-fifth hour.
A croaking cat.

I will put in the box . . .
A book made of water.
An elephant crossed with a cheetah.
An icicle made of grass.

My box is shaped with
Electricity and water.
The lock is made of fire.
In the corners it has rubies and sapphires.

I will jump in my box
On a golden trampoline
That will bounce forever.

Ross Payne (9)
Wilburton VPC School

The Magic Box

(Based on 'Magic Box' by Kit Wright)

I will put in the box . . .
Some sparkling stars from the shimmering blue sky
A fairy to give me my five wishes
All my friends so I can see them forever.

I will put in the box . . .
One bright blue horseshoe
A fabulous atmosphere with chocolate for air
My favourite destination Cuba - everywhere.

I will put in the box . . .
A pink fluffy dog with the weirdest bark
A lolly that tastes of fish and chips
The largest dolphin that covers the sea.

My box is created from crystals and diamonds
The lid is made of rubies
Its hinges are stems of flowers.

I will swim in my box
All the way to the sunset
Then come back home
And make a wish to see it all again.

Jennifer Weldon (10)
Wilburton VPC School

My Magic Box

(Based on 'Magic Box' by Kit Wright)

I will put in my box . . .
The glorious, glamorous goldfish
The whisper of wind in the west
The smell of the wonderful clouds.

I will put in my box . . .
The sprinkle and sparkle of the south
The greenest everlasting grass
A white, wise horse.

I will put in my box . . .
The souls of the sea
An iced up spider web
A little wave from the Indian Ocean.

My box is decorated with sequins and metal
With rubies on the lid
And all the winds in the corners.

I will dance the night away in my box
In Dancing Land
In moonlight.

Mellissa Binks (10)
Wilburton VPC School

My Magical Box

(Based on 'Magic Box' by Kit Wright)

I will put in the box . . .
A whisper from a dog in its sleep,
The last quack from a dying duck
And a magical guitar that makes a beautiful sound.

I will put in the box . . .
The first man on Mars
A creamy bite of a hot ice cream
And an everlasting pony ride.

I will put in the box . . .
The smallest house that I can grow
A flower with rubbery roots
And a newly laid egg from a dragon.

My box is made from a firefly
The lid and corners are silver
The lock is marble and the key is a bamboo stick.

I shall ride in my box
On the back of an elephant
To the rarest place on Earth
Then swim the longest lagoon
To the largest chocolate factory ever.

Anjela Griffiths (10)
Wilburton VPC School

My Magic Box

(Based on 'Magic Box' by Kit Wright)

I will put in my box . . .
The twist of the universe and its glory
The start of winter's breeze and white glorious snow
The sun of a hot summer's day.

I shall put in my box . . .
A lumber from a herd of purple dogs
A wish that will never end
A creamy bit of chocolate.

I would put in my box . . .
A wonderful dream in a comfortable bed
A song of praise to God
The first bark of Pipin my dog.

My box will be modelled of gold
And it will have a sign of secret
And stars in the corner.
The lock will be made of ink.

I will buy in my box
All the things I want.
Things no one else can buy
Only me and my key.

Josh Greene (9)
Wilburton VPC School

My Magic Box

(Based on 'Magic Box' by Kit Wright)

I will put in my box . . .
A dinosaur that would be my friend
And a meteor that travels everywhere
And an everlasting life.

I will put in my box . . .
A chocolate bar that never ends
A life that lasts forever.

I will put in my box . . .
A planet called Hide-and-Seek
And the highest mountain that never stops.

I shall put in my box . . .
Hundreds of gold bars
A mirror that can show the future.

My box is made from tar
With a gem cross in the middle
And with dinosaur skin on the cover.

I shall surf in my box
And wash up in Chocolate Land.

Harley Pyne (9)
Wilburton VPC School

My Magic Box

(Based on 'Magic Box' by Kit Wright)

I will put in the box . . .
The first cry of a baby and
The second egg of a dying dragon.

I will put in the box . . .
The wonderful noise of a dinosaur egg cracking.

I will put in the box . . .
The last laugh of a dying uncle
And a dream of a floating bird hitting the depths of the sea.

The box is made of gold, silver and in the corners myrrh.
I will travel back in time to see the wars and command them.

Philip Kirby (9)
Wilburton VPC School

Wiggles Milkshake Store

I am Wiggle Giggles,
I run Wiggles Milkshake Store,
There are flavours in my freezer,
You have never seen before,
9 sumptuous creations,
Too milky to resist,
Why not do yourself a flavour,
Try the flavours on my list.

Red blood drippy cream,
Carrot sun baked bream,
Watermelon drops, cabbaged plum,
Butter mustard, gravy gum,
Cotton onion, chocolate ham,
Candy sprout, pickle yam,
Pizza chew, potato dip,
Turnip strip, waffle flip,
Sour rhubarb, strawberry cheddar.

Stacey Lee George (9)
Winhills County Primary School

My Mother's Frog

My mother's frog is green and spotty,
My dad's snake is happy and potty.

My brother's hamster is big and bold,
My sister's mouse is skinny as a cloud.

My auntie's tortoise is slow and steady,
My uncle's parrot is cheeky and loud.

My grandma's dog is sillier than a frog,
My grandad's cat is brown like a hog.

Ayeshia Evans (9)
Winhills County Primary School

My Mother's Dog

My mother's dog is as brown as a hedgehog,
My brother's toy can run and jog.

My sister's hamster all grey and damp,
My dad's tools are all cramped.

My cousin's cat is big and fat,
My grandma's parrot is cocky and mean.

Sam Everett (8)
Winhills County Primary School

My Cousin's Dog

My cousin's dog is as thin as a hat,
My auntie's mouse is as fat as a cat.

My sister's hamster is as thin as me,
My brother's cat swallowed a key.

My uncle's hair got eaten by a bear,
My nanny's monkey has not one hair.

Peter Housden (7)
Winhills County Primary School

My Mum's Dog

My dad's tortoise is as fat as a pig,
My mum's hamster is bold and big.

My uncle's cow is as thin as a cat,
My gran's pig is as long as a sausage.

My auntie's cat is as thin as a tiger,
My grandad's muscles are as strong as a wrestler.

My brother's horse is as smelly as a pig,
My sister's dog is always barking.

Jack Hayward (7)
Winhills County Primary School

My Chocolate

Melty, sticky, minty chocolate,
Bars and bars of chocolate all mine, not yours,
I bet you're jealous because I've got all the chocolate.
Minty, delicious chocolate,
With light bubbles inside,
Jealous, jealous that's what you are,
Chocolate, chocolate is what I have.

Josh Hattle (11)
Winhills County Primary School

Cat

Mouse muncher
Tail chaser
Bird frightener
Soft pouncer
Sleek jumper
Miaow, miaow.

Vanessa Aveling (10)
Winhills County Primary School

The Storm

A multitude of gathering clouds,
Are appearing gradually,
Suddenly the sky grew black
And grey and gloomy,
Lightning strikes across the sky
And rain chucks it down,
I'm pleased I'm sitting inside
Warm and dry by the fireplace,
Soon the storm is gone
Because the clouds are floating away
And the sun is coming out.

Dale Banim (10)
Winhills County Primary School

Mrs Grandison

Mrs Grandison is a rocking chair,
She is a squeaky mouse,
A falcon swooping down to school,
A daffodil blowing in the wind,
She is the summer sun,
She is a San Francisco cocktail,
She is an athlete.

Ryan Whittingham (11)
Winhills County Primary School

A Rabbit

Furry hopper,
Carrot chewer,
Lettuce muncher,
Fluffy burrower,
Shy bounder.

Lauren Daye (11)
Winhills County Primary School

The Teacher

He's a bumpy bench,
He's a red baboon,
He's a speeding eagle,
A bouncing bluebell,
The noisy construction site,
A warm evening,
A glass of crackling Coke,
A builder.

Bobby Hubbard (10)
Winhills County Primary School

The Snail

Little, slimy, slow snails,
Move across the ground,
Eating leaves, dodging birds,
Moving for their lives,
Leaving long slimy trails,
Which my cat tries to follow,
It is definitely a hard job to be
A very slow snail.

Jonathan Huggett (10)
Winhills County Primary School

My Teacher

She's a big bouncy chair,
She's a huge grizzly bear,
She's a massive moody eagle,
She's a small pretty daffodil,
She is a mad professor,
She is this at lunchtime,
She is a Dr Pepper,
She is a mad archaeologist.

Matthew Beckett (10)
Winhills County Primary School

My Dad's Bear

My dad's bear is big and bold,
My mum's mouse is like a toad.

My nanny's bunny smells like tea,
My grandad's fish looks like a tee.

My uncle's sword is as sharp as steel,
My aunt's bag is like a meal.

My cousin's vote was three,
My sister's boat is a tree.

My auntie's toad is as green as a Christmas tree,
My fairy is just like me.

My pink panther's cat is as black as night,
My lion's dog gave it a fright and a bite.

Tiana Fabray-Smith (8)
Winhills County Primary School

My Dog

You cannot help but like
My little dog called Tyke.
With his long waggly tail
You couldn't possibly fail

He has a cheeky fluffy face
And he is always in disgrace
And when he goes to greet you
It looks like he's gonna eat you.

Because he can be very lovable
He can also be very huggable
And when he goes out
He cannot stop running about
And he barks, woof, woof, woof!

David Maddy (11)
Winhills County Primary School

Down Behind The Fish Bowl

Down behind the fish bowl,
I met a cat called Nasher,
'What are you doing?' he said,
'Just being a basher!'

Down behind the fish bowl,
I met a cat called Ted,
'What are you doing?' he said
'I'm just making my bed.'

Down behind the fish bowl,
I met a cat called Mat,
'What are you doing?' he said,
'Just looking at this bat.'

Timothy Franklin (10)
Winhills County Primary School

Emily

She is a soft bouncy bed.
She is a lonely cuddly dog.
She is a parrot yapping all the time.
She is a bright red poppy.
The sound of baby birds.
A reflection of the hot sun.
She's a juicy orange drink.
She's a careful beautician.
She is a hot spicy curry.
She's a tall, skinny birthday present.

Hayley Curtis (10)
Winhills County Primary School

The Writer Of This Poem

(Based on 'The Writer of this Poem' by Roger McGough)

The writer of this poem is Kirsty Carter.
As strong as Hulk Hogan.
As gentle as a baby.
As fast as a Olympic swimmer.
As slow as a tortoise
As happy as a dolphin
As silly as a clown.
As light as a feather.
As brave as a lion.
As still as a stone.
As pretty as an angel.

Kirsty Carter (9)
Winhills County Primary School

The Teacher

He's a big stiff chair
He's an enormous bee buzzing through the sky, ready to sting
A falcon flying and gliding hoping to find his prey
A big red rose bud with prickly thorns
A deep voice that echoes through the walls
A cloudy night
He's a pint of gin
An angry teacher growling through walls
He's burning hot and spicy chilli peppers
A cold winter breeze blowing up snow.

Liam Allen (11)
Winhills County Primary School

The Writer Of This Poem

(Based on 'The Writer of this Poem' by Roger McGough)

The writer of this poem is Bradley Winfield
As strong as the strongest men.
As gentle as a leaf.
As slow as a tortoise.
As happy as a joker.
As silly as a clown.
As smart as a teacher.
As cool as Jermain Defoe.
As fat as a pig.
As thin as a pancake.

Bradley Winfield (7)
Winhills County Primary School

My Teddy

My teddy chubby and fat,
Cuddly soft and quite a rat,
Plump on the inside,
Fluffy on the out,
Poor little teddy give me a shout
Brown patches on face,
Enormous nose, wonderful paws,
Loves to play, cute little teddy,
Give me a hug today.

Sophie Freeston (11)
Winhills County Primary School

Dalian

He is a single size bed, also bouncy.
He is a jumping kangaroo.
A pigeon getting trained.
A dandelion clock swaying in the breeze.
The sound of a beeping car.
He's the morning sunrise.
Appleade fizzing up and down.
A very funny comedian.
He's a sausage with tomato ketchup.
The summer with the golden sun.

Peter Curtis (11)
Winhills County Primary School

Teacher

She's a clean window always open.
A dog that's always playful and calm.
A sweet robin singing on a cold frosty day.
She's a bright yellow tulip swaying in the breeze.
The sound of a violin.
A summer's evening with children playing football.
A cold drink of Sunny D with ice cubes melting.
A teacher at a playgroup making everyone happy.
A melting pepperoni and cheese pizza.
She's a summer's day.

Zoe Leddy (10)
Winhills County Primary School

The Writer Of This Poem

(Based on 'The Writer of this Poem' by Roger McGough)

The writer of this poem is Billy.
As strong as a bulldozer.
As gentle as a feather.
As fast as a cheetah.
As slow as a snail.
As happy as a teddy.
As silly as a clown.
As tall as a pyramid.
As good as gold.
As fat as a pig.
As cool as an ice pop.

Billy Land (8)
Winhills County Primary School

My Teacher

He is a golden letterbox
He is a vicious tiger protecting his cubs
A barn owl scanning for mice above a cornfield
The scent of a mint
The roar of a tractor, starting up on a frosty morning
He is the first dawn of spring
A chocolate milkshake at McDonalds
He's a clown, telling jokes at a circus
He's a pepperoni pizza burning in the oven
He is a white Christmas.

Lauren Goldsmith (11)
Winhills County Primary School

Yummy

I am Harry Barry,
I run Harry Barry's Chocolate Store,
There are flavours in my mixture,
You have never seen before.
Seven lovely creations,
Too rummy scrummy to resist,
Why not do yourself a favour,
Try the flavour on my list:

Choc chip broccoli cake,
Yummy, scrummy as I bake,
Carrot apple crumble,
As my tummy rumbles.
Sour apple pie,
Is what people like to buy,
Cookie with pasta chips,
As they put it near their lips,
Custard brown spice on top,
Bubbling now, it's going to pop,
Onion dumpling, doble dip,
Turnip truffle triple flip,
Chocolate custard, yummy, yummy,
As they put it near their tummy.

I am Harry Barry,
I run Harry's Chocolate Store
Taste a flavour from my mixture,
You will surely ask for more.

Rhianon Smith (9)
Winhills County Primary School

The Writer Of This Poem

(Based on 'The Writer of this Poem' by Roger McGough)

The writer of this poem is Holly Freeston.
As strong as Superman.
As gentle as a bunny.
As fast as the wind.
As slow as a slug.
As happy as a smile.
As silly as a joke.
As cute as an angel.
As angry as a devil.
As scary as a haunted house.
As healthy as a doctor.

Holly Freeston (9)
Winhills County Primary School

The Writer Of This Poem

(Based on 'The Writer of this Poem' by Roger McGough)

The writer of this poem is Dean Allen.
As strong as a bulldozer.
As gentle as a feather
As fast as a cheetah.
As slow as a snail.
As happy as God.
As silly as a clown.
As cool as a Nissan skyline.
As tall as a pyramid.
As good as gold.
As fat as a pig.

Dean Allen (7)
Winhills County Primary School

My Teacher

She is a bright red cupboard door, always open.
She is a preying cat.
An eagle flying around the sky.
The smell of a rose.
The sound of a woodpecker.
A crystal morning.
A sparkling soda.
A foster parent.
A white chocolate bar.
She is a hot summer's day.

Adam Townsend (10)
Winhills County Primary School

My Teacher

He's a cold wooden chair.
A wasp buzzing through the air.
A big rosebush in the way.
A loud sound echoing through the walls.
A cold winter's night.
A bottle of fizzy drink
And a hard-working teacher.
Red hot chilli peppers.
A winter blizzard.

Mark Everett (10)
Winhills County Primary School

Tiger

Fluffy fluffer,
Pouncing pouncer,
Red-blood killer,
Orange cruncher,
Roaring roarer,
Stripy tearer.

Mollie Fleming (10)
Winhills County Primary School

Jessie The Tale Of Bog
(A cautionary tale, written in the style of Hilaire Belloc and Heinrich Hoffmann)

My best friend knew a boy called Bog
Who never stopped eating the hairs of his dog.
On the fourth day he had stomach ache
He felt really ill for goodness sake.
When it was night he went to bed
But didn't wake up because he was dead.

Jessie Meeds (7)
Winhills County Primary School

The Tragic Tale Of Big Jack
(A cautionary tale written in the style of Hilaire Belloc and Heinrich Hoffmann)

Eating too many biscuits was what Jack did all day,
Jack was a skinny lad
Whose habit was extremely bad.
He ate biscuits all the day
Then in his bay he went to lay.
He went and sat on his bed
When Mum and Dad came up he was dead.

Jack Housden (9)
Winhills County Primary School

The Tale Of Lee
(A cautionary tale written in the style of Hilaire Belloc and Heinrich Hoffmann)

The boy who ate fleas and bees.
The young boy Lee ate some bees,
'Yummy I really like these!'
Then the sting began at his knees
And worked up to his head where he had fleas.
The moral of the story you see
Is just to eat what Mum gives you for tea.

Nathan Lee George (7)
Winhills County Primary School

The Writer Of This Poem

My dad is handsome as can be.
My uncle is as clever as can be.
My brother is a pain.
My mum is pretty as can be.
My auntie is wonderful as can be.
All my cousins are small.
My dog is beautiful.
My fish is nice.
My snake is a pain.
My tortoise is slow coach.
My turtle likes swimming in water.
My puppy is quiet.
My guard dog is tough, rough.
When I was a baby I looked lovely.

Megan Hayward (7)
Winhills County Primary School

The Tale Of Meg The Girl Who Ate Egg Shell
(A cautionary tale written in the style of Hilaire Belloc and Heinrich Hoffmann)

Meg was healthy, had good friends
She rode her bike fast round bends.
Bullies convinced her to eat egg shell
She ate some shell, whizzed round and rang the bell.
She got some shell stuck in her throat.
There she sounded like a Billy goat.
She went up to her lonely bed,
And on the eighth day she was dead.

Megan Moles (8)
Winhills County Primary School

The Writer Of This Poem

(Based on 'The Writer of this Poem' by Roger McGough)

The writer of this poem is Stuart Chamberlain.
As strong as a rock.
As gentle as a feather.
As fast as a cheetah.
As slow as a snail.
As happy as a happy Christmas.
As silly as a clown.
As rich as a king.
As still as a clock.
As girlie as Mr Stealy.
As hot as Kenya.

Stuart Chamberlain (7)
Winhills County Primary School

The Tale Of Meg Who Eats Too Much Raw Egg

(A cautionary tale written in the style of Hilaire Belloc and Heinrich Hoffmann)

There was once a little girl called Meg,
Who ate big bits of raw egg.
When she had finished she went to bed
And one had gone up into her head.
In the morning she went into her shed,
She died in there because of what I've said.
The little girl who ate eggs that were raw,
Is no more!

Megan Baumert (7)
Winhills County Primary School

The Writer Of This Poem

(Based on 'The Writer of this Poem' by Roger McGough)

The writer of this poem is Ben Cooper.
As strong as King-Kong.
As gentle as a flower.
As fast as a plane.
As slow as a snail.
As happy as a chick.
As silly as a clown.
As carnivorous as a T-Rex.
As thin as a worm.
As fat as an elephant.
As cool as Robbie Williams.

Ben Cooper (8)
Winhills County Primary School

My Friend Peter

He is a bouncy king-size bed.
He's a rolling bulldog that never stops.
He is a parrot that never stops talking.
The scent of a poppy.
The sound of thunder and lightning.
He is a car going to work.
A fizzy drink.
He's a builder making a house.
He's a roast chicken.
The sun in the sky.

Dalian White (10)
Winhills County Primary School

The Writer Of This Poem

(Based on 'The Writer of this Poem' by Roger McGough)

The writer of this poem is Leah Fowles.
As strong as a lion.
As gentle as a feather.
As fast as a cheetah.
As slow as a snail.
As happy as a rainbow.
As silly as a clown.
As healthy as a fruit.
As frightening as a ghost.
As good as an angel.
As angry as a frown.

Leah Fowles (9)
Winhills County Primary School

Horses

Kindly canterer,
Graceful galloper,
Beautiful trotter,
Wonderful walker,
Vegetable eater,
Broccoli muncher,
Potato cruncher,
Water swallower,
Galloping jumper.

Laura Donelan (10)
Winhills County Primary School

The Writer Of This Poem

(Based on 'The Writer of this Poem' By Roger McGough)

The writer of this poem is Rhys Williams.
As strong as a gorilla.
As gentle as a tree.
As fast as a cheetah.
As slow as a sloth.
As happy as a chicken.
As silly as a joker.
As big as a blue whale.
As small as an ant.
As cool as Mr Stealy.
As good as gold.

Rhys Williams (9)
Winhills County Primary School

The Writer Of This Poem

(Based on 'The Writer of this Poem' by Roger McGough)

The writer of this poem is Taylor Grimes.
As strong as a lion man.
As gentle as a feather.
As fast as a cheetah.
As slow as a snail.
As happy as Christmas.
As silly as a clown.
As quiet as a stone.
As cool as an ice lolly.
As quick as a kick.
As bouncy as a rabbit.

Taylor Grimes (7)
Winhills County Primary School

The Writer Of This Poem

(Based on 'The Writer of this Poem' by Roger McGough)

The writer of this poem
Is a freaky as can be.

As smelly as a belly,
As wibbly as a welly.

As strong as a brick,
As quick as a stick.

As fast as a busy bee,
As gentle as a dizzy flea.

As slow as a slug,
As cuddly as a rug.

Danielle Jones (8)
Winhills County Primary School

The Writer Of This Poem

(Based on 'The Writer of this Poem' by Roger McGough)

The writer of this poem is Skye Banim.
As strong as a wrestler.
As gentle as a mouse.
As fast as a cheetah.
As slow as a turtle.
As happy as a best friend.
As silly as Billy.

Skye Banim (8)
Winhills County Primary School

The Writer Of This Poem

(Based on 'The Writer of this Poem' by Roger McGough)

The writer of this poem is Jack Wheeler.
As strong as a box.
As gentle as a mouse.
As fast as a Lamborghini.
As slow as a tortoise.
As happy as a joker.
As silly as a monkey.
As funny as a clown.
As quick as a cat.
As slow as a pencil.
As cool as David Beckham.

Jack Wheeler (8)
Winhills County Primary School

The Writer Of This Poem

(Based on 'The Writer of this Poem' by Roger McGowan)

The writer of this poem is Lauren Sharp.
As strong as a weightlifter.
As gentle as a dove.
As fast as a cheetah.
As slow as a snail.
As happy as can be.
As silly as a clown.
As still as a house.
As quiet as a mouse.
As bright as the sun.
As pale as a ghost.

Lauren Sharp (8)
Winhills County Primary School

The Writer Of This Poem

(Based on 'The Writer of this Poem' by Roger McGough)

The writer of this poem is Annie Cerveno.
As strong as a rock.
As gentle as a feather.
As fast as a cheetah.
As slow as a snail.
As happy as a happy Christmas.
As silly as a clown.
As rich as the king.
As still as a block.
As girlie as Mr Stealy.
As hot as Kenya.

Annie Cerveno (7)
Winhills County Primary School

The Writer Of This Poem

(Based on 'The Writer of this Poem' by Roger McGough)

The writer of this poem is Rebecca Kane.
As strong as the strongest man in the world.
As gentle as a feather.
As fast as a cheetah.
As slow as a snail.
As happy as a teddy bear.
As silly as a clown.
As blue as the ocean.
As fat as a pig.
As good as an angel.
As small as a crumb.

Rebecca Kane (7)
Winhills County Primary School

The Writer Of This Poem
(Based on 'The Writer of this Poem' by Roger McGough)

The writer of this poem
Is thinner than a pig,
As strong as a brick,
As gentle as fur,
As fast as a monkey.

As slow as a snail,
As happy as a laughing clown,
As silly as a dog.

As colourful as a rainbow,
As funny as a monkey,
As sensible as a girl,
As healthy as a life that never dies.

As busy as a bee,
As hot as a fire,
And me who believes in every way
And always loves to read
And loves to sleep, she loves her sleep,
Or so this poem says.

Jade Sutherley (8)
Winhills County Primary School

The Writer Of This Poem
(Based on 'The Writer of this Poem' by Roger McGough)

The writer of this poem,
Is as kind as can be,
As strong as a brick,
As gentle as a butterfly,
As smooth as a dolphin,
As colourful as a rainbow,
As bright as the sun,
As smiley as a face,
As funny as a monkey.

Mica Webster (8)
Winhills County Primary School

The Writer Of This Poem

(Based on 'The Writer of this Poem' by Roger McGough)

The writer of this poem,
Is as fast as lightning,
As strong as a dinosaur,
As cheeky as a chimpanzee,
As clever as a parrot,
As yummy as a cake,
As heavy as a giant,
As blue as the Indian Ocean,
As silly as a comedian,
As hot as a desert,
As bright as the sun,
As funny as a clown,
As naughty as a mime.

Lee Davis (7)
Winhills County Primary School

The Writer Of This Poem

(Based on 'The Writer of this Poem' by Roger McGough)

The writer of this poem is red as a rose,
As strong as a man,
As gentle as a brick.

As fast as a car,
As slow as a slug,
As happy as a liver,
As silly as can be.

As mean as a bear,
As tall as a tree.

Lucy Webb (7)
Winhills County Primary School

The Writer Of This Poem

(Based on 'The Writer of this Poem' by Roger McGough)

The writer of this poem
Is cool as a kangaroo,
As strong as metal,
As gentle as can be,
As slow as a snail,
As silly as a cup,
As fast as a Maclaren
As bold as a hen,
As cool as a pop star,
As hot as a radiator.

Giovanni Chinnici (8)
Winhills County Primary School

The Writer Of This Poem

(Based on 'The Writer of this Poem' by Roger McGough)

The writer of this poem,
Is as beautiful as a butterfly,
As strong as a giant,
As gentle as a frog.

As fast as a cheetah,
As slow as a giraffe,
As happy as a clown,
As silly as can be,
As wonderful as an angel.

April Collingwood (8)
Winhills County Primary School

The Writer Of This Poem
(Based on 'The Writer of this Poem' by Roger McGough)

The writer of this poem is
As fat as can be,
As strong as a boxer,
As gentle as can be,
As fast as a jet,
As slow as an ant,
As silly as a monkey,
As funny as a clown,
As silly as Mark,
As good as gold,
As spooky as a bat.

Mark Bailey (8)
Winhills County Primary School

The Writer Of This Poem
(Based on 'The Writer of this Poem' by Roger McGough)

The writer of this poem is
As good as gold,
As stinky as a sock,
As grubby as a cake,
As slow as a snail,
As fast as a fish,
As soft as a hamster,
As rough as a hedgehog.

Leon Criddle (8)
Winhills County Primary School

The Writer Of This Poem
(Based on 'The Writer of this Poem' by Roger McGough)

The writer of this poem
Is as pretty as a butterfly,
As bright as the moon,
As light as a feather.

As fast as a shooting star,
As gentle as a bee,
As silly as a clown,
As smooth as a dolphin.

As strong as a wall,
As sweet as a lolly,
As little as a mouse,
As tall as a tree.

Shannon Charter (8)
Winhills County Primary School

The Writer Of This Poem
(Based on 'The Writer of this Poem' by Roger McGough)

The writer of this poem is as good as can be,
As strong as a dragon,
As gentle as a bird,
As fast as a car,
As slow as a snail,
As happy as can be,
As silly as an ape,
As small as a bush,
As colourful as a rainbow,
As slippery as a jellyfish.

Sarah-Jane Rawlinson (8)
Winhills County Primary School

The Writer Of This Poem

(Based on 'The Writer of this Poem' by Roger McGough)

The writer of this poem is,
As funky as a flower,
As strong as a train,
As gentle as can be,
As fast as a plane,
As slow as a turtle,
As happy as a cat,
As silly as a clown,
As pretty as a dog,
As good as gold,
As soft as silk,
As tame as a fox,
Or so the poem says.

Sofie Keddie (8)
Winhills County Primary School

The Writer Of This Poem

(Based on 'The Writer of this Poem' by Roger McGough)

The writer of this poem is
As clever as a monkey,
As strong as an elephant,
As gentle as a fish,
As fast as a cheetah,
As slow as a mouse,
As happy as can be,
As silly as a monkey.

Andrew Gosnall (9)
Winhills County Primary School

The Writer Of This Poem
(Based on 'The Writer of this Poem' by Roger McGough)

The writer of this poem is
Funnier than a comedian,
As strong as a black hole,
As gentle as an ant,
As fast as a greyhound,
As slow as a slug,
As happy as a goldfish in its new tank,
As silly as a clown.

As tall as a skyscraper,
As fat as an elephant,
Skinnier than a rope,
As good as sunshine.

Marc Hills (8)
Winhills County Primary School

The Writer Of This Poem
(Based on 'The Writer of this poem' by Roger McGough)

The writer of this poem,
Is as smart as a brain,
As strong as a rock,
As gentle as a rabbit.

As fast as mice,
As slow as snails,
As funny as a clown,
As keen as an ocean,
As sharp as a nib
Or so the poem says.

Liam Surkitt (7)
Winhills County Primary School

The Writer Of This Poem

(Based on 'The Writer of this Poem' by Roger McGough)

The writer of this poem,
Is cheekier than a monkey,
As strong as a boxer,
As gentle as can be,
As fast as a horse,
As slow as an ant,
As happy as a crab,
As silly as a parrot,
As lucky as a cheetah,
Brainier than a brainiac,
As colourful as a rainbow.

Curtis Bundy (9)
Winhills County Primary School

The Tooth

My tooth is wobbly I want to take it out.
I wiggle it and jiggle it and move it all about.
I wiggle it till it pops out of my gum
I just want to show my mum.
I put the tooth at night in my bed
The fairy comes and lifts up my head.
She takes the tooth and leaves a pound
She does not even make a sound.
In the morning I wake up and see
A pound under my pillow just for me.

Sophie Paveling (8)
Wittering Primary School

Webster The Spider

W ebster the spider eats lots of flies,
E ach time he doesn't catch some he cries and cries,
B ut Ellie the spider she lives in our mugs,
S he's caught so many more tiny poor bugs,
T hen Webster gets jealous he puts on a face,
E llie the spider she wins first place,
R ight now Webster thinks she's a disgrace.

T hey've settled for friends it's ok with me,
H e doesn't enjoy it but it impresses Ellie,
E ating a fly he suddenly said, 'Sorry but I need to go to bed.'

S o Ellie and Webster, enemies now,
P eople split up after one simple row,
I think it was wrong they shouldn't off split,
D o you agree but he was just saying sit?
E llie the spider won second place,
R ight now she thinks Webster's the disgrace.

Jessica-Leigh White (8)
Wittering Primary School

The Treasure Chest

Deep beneath a chimney sweep,
The treasure lies beneath his feet.
Under floorboards, under dust,
There's the treasure full of mould and rust.
In the chest is a shiny gold penny,
It's worth millions but there's not many.
If these people realise why,
Their squeaky floorboards sound so high.
They will never know that the chest is there,
And if they do, then be*ware!*

Carris Boast (11)
Wittering Primary School

The Bay Mustang

She galloped across the canyon grass
And trotted till the sun ray passed,
She lolloped on, jumping over the two metre stones,
But one day she ran past yellow cones.
Next thing she knew, she was in a large ring,
Suddenly there came a loud, *bring, bring*.
Then came a man and jumped on her back,
She bucked and her hooves crashed into a haystack.
But finally she threw him away,
She galloped over the fence, and past the hay.
She carried on cantering till she found a lake,
She drank and drank till that was all she could take.
The last I saw of her was when she was grazing by the hill,
When everything was quiet and so still.

Siobhan Bishop (10)
Wittering Primary School

Too Many Animals

Mum can I please get a dog?
I know I've already got one but he just chews his log.

Mum can I please have a cat?
I know we've got one but he just sits on the mat.

Mum can we please get a budgie?
I know Dad's got one but his just sleeps in the study.

Mum can we please get a snake?
I know Ryan's got one but his just sits by his backyard lake.

Mum can we please get a pet?
But her response was, 'Not yet!'

Darcy Owen (10)
Wittering Primary School

Football Crazy

F ans gather for the match,
O n the day the tickets are sold,
O ff of the benches and in the ground,
T ables of merchandise all around,
B anging on the seat in front,
A ll of the fans are excited,
L oads of players warming up,
L ighted flares everywhere.

C ool breeze in the stand,
R unning onto the pitch, kick-off time,
A   goal, I don't believe it!
Z illions of fans cheer and shout
Y es, our team has scored!

One-Nil

Jack Yule (9)
Wittering Primary School

The Life Of My Candle

My little candle so red and round,
Sat in the cupboard lost but now found.
I took it out and lit it one night
And I watched the flames burning so bright.
I watched the flames flickering away,
This is lovely, as I would say.
The wax had melted and formed a pool,
I picked it up when it was hard and cool.
The wick went out, my candle was flat
So in the cupboard I put it back.

Emma Elks (11)
Wittering Primary School

My Dad

When my dad went away,
I cried and cried and cried,
When my dad went away.

He was gone for ages,
We thought he might not come back,
Then we were told he was missing.

One day we heard the doorbell,
I went and opened it,
And there was my dad!

I cried and cried and cried,
But this time,
This time of happiness.

Amber Cooper (10)
Wittering Primary School

Emotions

Emotions are feelings,
Emotions are like paint peeling,
One day they're up high,
Next they're saying goodbye,
Happiness is like joy,
Sadness is when you get dumped by a boy,
Laughter is when you're happy inside,
Anger is when a relative died,
That's what emotions are!

Katie Evans (10)
Wittering Primary School

The Kitten

One fine day we went out to get,
A nice big cuddly, brand new pet.

We went to shops, rescue centres and much more,
Until we found what we were looking for.

A bungalow which had kittens for sale,
We all cried to Mum with a wail.

We all imagined cute little things with paws,
We wanted a look so we went indoors.

As we wiped our feet on the mat we saw,
Something that made us stare in awe.

All curled up around the fire,
Was something we would all desire.

A little kitten all cute and round,
So we paid the lady exactly five pound.

As soon as we got through the front door,
We could hardly believe what we saw.

The little kitten's eyes turned red,
And started to tear up Mother's bed.

It ran around the kitchen and ate,
All the scraps of food that were on the plates.

Mum then screamed, 'Let's take it back,'
She then threw the kitten into a sack.

She drove and drove in the car,
Until she was somewhere very far!

She threw the kitten into a well,
Into the well the kitten fell.

So the evil kitten went away then,
But back to the pet shop for us again.

Emily Allison (11)
Wittering Primary School

Animal Antics

On Monday, my dog died,
I cried and cried and cried.
Oh, it was so bad and it was so sad,
On Monday my dog died.

On Tuesday my cat ran away,
I didn't know what to say.
Oh, it wasn't that nice and it's happened twice,
On Tuesday my cat ran away.

On Wednesday my hamster was sold,
It made me a lot less bold.
Oh, the woman who got him, she named him Jim,
On Wednesday my hamster was sold.

On Thursday my horse got lost
And for a new one you should see the cost.
Oh, now no riding school and that was cool,
On Thursday my horse got lost.

On Friday my tortoise hibernated,
I waited and waited and waited.
Oh, I put him in the shed, which is now his bed,
On Friday my tortoise hibernated.

On Saturday my rabbit gave birth,
But then burrowed into the earth,
Oh, I was so sad but yet so mad!
On Saturday my rabbit gave birth.

On Sunday no pets I had!
In which I told my dad!
He spent all his money and got me a bunny
On Sunday *one* pet I had.

Bethany Giddings (11)
Wittering Primary School

My Family

My mum's crystal ball shines so bright,
But it doesn't sparkle in the middle of the night.
My dad's wallet has many things,
Some money, a credit card and some keyrings.
My sister's books have many pages,
She could sit down and read for ages.
My brother's toys crash and clang,
When we are silent he makes a big bang.
My heart has a warm and cuddly touch,
But no one seems to like it much.
My family is always there for me,
They are so kind but it's just hard to see.

Louise Paveling (11)
Wittering Primary School

Sickerling

There was an old man from Wick
That was born in a puddle of sick
He had a body of a snake
And a head of a rake
So his mum decided to chuck him in a lake!

There was an old lady from Waterloo
That had a whale called Shamoo
He ate so much meat,
That he couldn't compete
So he had to spend all the time in the loo!

Bethan Boast (9)
Wittering Primary School

I'm Not A Poet

I stare at the page before me,
All blank and clean and new.
Hmmm, what should I put . . . ?
Oh, I'll have to scrap this poem too.

Oh, you see the rhythm doesn't work,
The rhyme does - only just,
Why can't I click my fingers and
But I can't think of a rhyme for just!

I'll never win the prize
That everyone wants to win.
Everyone else's working so hard . . .
Something, something, something pin.

Oh I'm fed up of writing poems,
I'm just so rubbish and
Now everyone else is finished,
They're getting experiments planned.

Oh look, oh look, oh look!
I've finally made a rhyme.
I thought that when I started
I'd run right out of time.

But . . . when I read it again and again
Because I'm supposed to check it,
It makes me feel fed up
And sort of pathetic.

I'll never win the prize,
That everyone wants to win.
This'll have to do for now . . .
Oh I still can't rhyme with win!

Eleanor Cradwick (10)
Wittering Primary School

The Charge Of The Mouse Brigade

(Based on 'The Charge of the Light Brigade' by Alfred Lord Tennyson)

Half an inch, half an inch,
Half an inch onward,
Into Cat Valley,
Rode the six hundred,
'Forward the Mouse Brigade!
Ravage their fleas!' he said,
'Capture the cheese!' he said.

Mouse trap to the right of them,
Mouse trap to the left of them,
Mouse trap in front of them,
Snapp'd and miaow'd,
Pounced on with cat and claws,
They ran into the pusses' paws,
Into the jaws of puss,
Into the mouth of sores,
Rode the six hundred.

Flash'd all their spears bare,
Flash'd as they squealed in the air,
Spearing all the pusses there,
Scampering an army while,
All the house wondered,
Plunged right into the fight,
Right thro' those teeth so white,
Ginger and Tabby,
Reel'd from the courage and might,
Shatter'd and sunder'd,
Then they rode back, but not
Not the six hundred.

Sarah Rouse (11)
Wittering Primary School

The Charge Of The Mouse Brigade

(Based on 'The Charge of the Light Brigade' by Alfred Lord Tennyson)

Half an inch, half an inch,
Half an inch onward,
Into Cat Valley,
Rode the six hundred.
'Forward the Mouse Brigade!
Ravage their fleas!' he said.
'Capture the cheese!' he said.

Claw to the right of them,
Claw to the left of them,
Claw in front of them,
Slash'd and scratch'd
They came like a knife to the throat.
Loud they did squeak to death,
Into the traps of cat,
Into the jaw of cat,
Rode the six hundred.

Flicked their tails here,
Flashed their collars bare,
Sobering the creatures were.
Bang from the front door,
In came a human to see,
Their cats guarding the mouldy cheese.
Out came a broom and away it flicked
Then they rode back but not,
Not the six hundred.

Hannah Guildford (10)
Wittering Primary School

Faulty Animals

I've got a new snake called Slip,
Who's always having a kip,
I sleep on the sofa,
While he devours a gopher,
So I want an ant called Dip.

I've got a new ant called Big
And once I fed him some fig,
He got bigger and bigger,
And started bouncing like Tigger,
So I want a horse called Wig.

I've got a new horse called Jane,
Who has a really long mane,
I make it look nice,
But she just chases mice,
So I want a dog called Dane.

I've got a new dog called Cane
Who just drives me to the insane
He's not very good,
He's always covered with blood
So I've got an imaginary friend called Norbet.

Alicia Tremlett (11)
Wittering Primary School

My Birds

Bobby and Hobby are my birds
Flying around making first words
Bob flies to his mirror and holds on tight
Saying, 'Come on Bob, you're all right.'
Hob raises his voice and sings a fine song
So good you'll want to sing along.

Frances Bannister (7)
Wittering Primary School

Nature

Lava in the volcano,
Water in the sea,
Mud in the ground,
Life in me.

Scent in the flower,
Honey in the beehive,
Softness in the tissue,
Sound in the music.

Joe Dame (7)
Wittering Primary School

My Mum Is . . .

My mum is *tall*
And can *stretch* up high
She has *long* brown hair
And *big* blue eyes
She does nice things for us all
And I love her more and more.

Mitchell Ansell (9)
Wittering Primary School